TELL THEM FOR ME

Mary Pat Kelly Upright

PAGE PUBLISHING, INC.
New York, NY

First originally published by Page Publishing, Inc. 2017

ISBN 978-1-63568-387-5 (Paperback)
ISBN 978-1-63568-388-2 (Digital)

Printed in the United States of America

I dedicate this book to my children Arika and John, and to my grandchildren, Nick, Luke and Ava. Pursue your dreams, be happy, and stay healthy in body, mind, and spirit. No words can express my love for you. Thanks for being you.

One of my greatest blessings in this world is that I am loved by you.

Next, I also dedicate this book to my siblings children. The love you gave my brothers and sisters completed them.

Thank you.

Nancy and Keith
Rikki, Diana, and Lee
Shannon, Brian, and Ashley
Jackie, Bobby, David, Deanna
Laurie, Corey, Jimmy, Shannon, Chris

Thanks for the part of life you fulfilled for us, and for loving us in spite of our brokenness. God bless you all.

Finally, I dedicate this book to my nieces and nephews from the wonderful families I was graced to be part of,

You're in my heart. God bless you always.

Renaye and Greg
Lisa and Todd
Aaron and Spike
Christa
Christine and Derek
Melissa
Wil and Tyler
Erika and Chandra
Bill, Bobby, and Lauren

I remember you with a grateful heart. Thank you. God bless your journey in life.

Desiderata… Jesus is Lord.

*We live our lives as a tale that is told. Therefore teach us to
number our days that we may incline our hearts unto wisdom.*

—*Psalm 90, KJV*

*There is a language within me; words waiting to
be spoken by Someone more Holy than I.*

This is my story. My story is no more important than your story.

I hope mine inspires you to tell yours, to remind you who you are.

The page was blank before her. Yet she knew there was something within her to say—something within her that had to be said, had to be written; something that had to be typed on the white blank sheets. The blank sheets, which would evolve into words that appeared to blossom out of the center of a seed, tightly bound then suddenly forming into a perfectly exotic flower. Stiff at first, tight, not so pretty, not so colorful or alive—then suddenly becoming a "breathtaking shape," exploding with color, a message from the heart of the master. The seed representing the brokenness of her journey that molded her into who she is today and why she had to write, why she must fill these empty pages and put on paper those silent conversations of her mind. Nothing defined—then suddenly growing, sprouting, taking shape into a perfectly well-told story. Hadn't it always been within her, her story? Those silent conversations in her head—weren't they, in fact, practiced lines of some chapter in some book not yet written, her book, her story? Yes, they were; she knew it. And she had carried them in the womb of her soul, waiting for their birth, waiting for them to come forth—waiting for the due time to turn the unseen into the seen, the intangible into the tangible, the ghost into the book. This was the time she was ready to say the words, *Tell Them for Me,* to tell her story.

Sixty years later and a lifetime lived, the story comes to the blank pages. Life's experiences on one tapestry, recording a life as a tale that is told. Here is part of mine. I hope it adds life to yours.

CHAPTER 1

THE FUNERAL WAS OVER, BUT the grief was not. Mary Pat walked the Main Street of the small upstate New York village with a deep sense of loss, drifting in and out of the reality that Brian would not be coming home. He was dead. Sometimes she accepted that fact and forged forward; other times the loss felt crippling. In those times, the grief washed over her like waves of an ocean. She had come to understand that's how it was with death and its loss. The tide of pain would come in and then recede, next time not catching her so off guard. Yet the reality of his death was something never too far from her. She walked recalling. The black wall phone—with a face plate that you dialed digit by digit in circular motion, with an extension cord that kept you by the phone not remotely wandering through the house—rang. It was 1970.

Her sister Sarra was on the other end. "Hello."

"Mary Pat, are you alone?"

"No, Mom's here, why, what's the matter?"

Mary Pat could hear in her sister's voice something was wrong.

"I have bad news for you, and I didn't want you to be there alone."

Anxious, she said, "I'm not alone, what's going on?"

"I hate to be the one telling you this, but Brian was killed in Vietnam on October 4. His mother wanted me to call you and said to tell you that they will be shipping his body back to the States, and it could take up to a week, but they will let you know when his body arrives in Carbondale."

"WHAT! WHAT DID YOU SAY? WHAT DID YOU SAY? WHAT? NO! NO! NO! No, IT CAN'T BE! NO! WHAT DID YOU SAY?"

Shock took over. Mary Pat could not process what she heard. She could not accept the reality of the words her sister was saying. Nothing felt real. Time and space melted away; a fog came over her, like a bubble around her, distancing her from air and breath. A deep core sadness strangled her heart as if she was in the grips of someone stopping her ability to breathe in and then out and then in. After the initial shock and recognition of what she had heard, Mary Pat operated in a numb state of being. Was there a mistake? Was it really Brian? Maybe they made a mistake. Maybe they confused him for someone else? Maybe he was alive really. Maybe he was alive. Maybe they got it all wrong. Maybe... maybe he would come home alive. These were her thoughts. They raced through her cognition. For the following week, she lived in the memories that she and Brian shared, oblivious to anything else functioning outside of the unseen bubble around her. She was cased in by this unseen presence, holding her at bay from the pain that wanted to devour her. How could this be? Brian. Not Brian. No, not Brian.

Her heart recalled his presence, always his presence. When she was afraid, alone, scared, abandoned, bad, sad—his presence always showed up, redirected, guided, comforted her. How would she live now without him? She was waiting, waiting for his body, waiting for the call that he was back on American soil, waiting for his viewing. What a terrible thought. How could she stand not seeing him move? How would she handle that she couldn't feel his warmth and hear his chuckle and see his sweet grin? That's warped—the thought of no life in a body that was so filled with life, lying there not moving, just lying there. It just did not compute in her thinking. It just could not be. She remembered the first time she heard about him. The older girls on the school bus were chattering delightfully over these new boys in town, these Upright boys. The air was all abuzz over the new family that moved into town with "good-looking sons"—all of whom would be riding their school bus! Oh, the joy! Brian was the oldest son, then Bradley, then Brent, and two younger siblings, Brett and Brenda, who were still too little to be on their bus. Brent became her "first kiss," playing spin the bottle on a big rock behind their house! The girls were crazy about those boys, rightfully so. They were great guys, raised in a good home, with good parents.

They were all nice, but Brian was special. He was a deep thinker. Even as a kid, he thought cautiously, was curious, and saw beyond the immediate—which isn't typical for teenage thinking. He was caring. If you looked into his eyes, he seemed to have a secret in his soul, like he knew something bigger than us but couldn't yet say what it was. When Mary Pat met Brian, he was everything and more than the girls on the bus predicted. He was different. He was so present; he was almost too good to be true. He was like that.

Brian became best friends with Mary Pat's older brother Gandy—which meant Mary Pat had the benefit of having Brian closer to her than he was to the other girls. They became good friends. Brian was there in the middle of her world, in the middle of the nightmare she lived in at her house. He witnessed the abuse. He felt the fear. He heard the craziness from the stepfather that dominated the atmosphere—a stepfather that groomed his victims until he caught whoever he was after, including Mary Pat's mother, Dorothy.

So after the initial grooming that set the stage for the abuse that was ahead, Merlin turned into a man who was to be feared and not trusted. His talk was smooth; his truth was vile. The family learned to tiptoe, as if it were walking on broken glass, ready to cut at any step taken, treading on thin ice that could crack and drown its victim any second. Caution was used constantly, always having to be on guard, never being able to just trust the environment, but rather daily watching, waiting, for the snake to come out of the wall and bite.

As a child and a young teen, Mary Pat never had a secure environment called home. There was no safe place, no safe nest, no one to go to who protected her. No, it was definitely not a safe home; it was a place filled with great anxiety for Mary Pat and her siblings. All Dorothy's children were neglected, abandoned, and abused in one form or another by this man who came into their lives as stepfather, and Brian watched it all.

Now, with his move into the little country town, there was someone who came as a light to her dark place. Brian was the good in her life. Brian had a girlfriend, and Mary Pat had a boyfriend—childhood crushes. It didn't stop either of them from becoming best friends. Brian always told Mary Pat he loved her. Riding the same school bus together every school day, he would remind her in his charming boyish way how much he cared about her.

Once, when Mary Pat was swearing and acting like a jerk to another girl on the bus, it was Brian who scolded her about it—chiding her for her actions and language, mildly reminding her how unbecoming it is to a girl to use foul language and unfair ridicule. She never smoked cigarettes because of him; she wanted him to be proud of her. She knew it would hurt him if she smoked, so it was easy not to. He was the one person in the world who believed in her. She didn't want to let him down. His presence kept her away from those outward things that could harm her inward beauty. He guided her, guarded her, and cared for her feelings. Brian loved Mary Pat, and she loved him. There was something ethereal about their friendship. Once, when Gandy and Brian were playing in the apple orchard in the trees near their home, Mary Pat joined to watch the boys play rodeo. The boys were climbing the apple trees then dropping onto the back of the cows under the tree and riding 'til they fell off. Mary Pat climbed the tree but didn't join in the game of riding the cows. She was laughing at these young boys owning their courage and risk, when her mother called from the house, "Maarrrreeee."

Mary Pat started frantically down from the apple tree. In haste she slipped and fell, falling to the ground. She landed faceup, looking upward into the underside of the apple leaves; she hit her head. Stunned, she still heard echoing, "Run, Mary, run!" It was Brian. A cow was galloping toward the tree's base exactly where Mary Pat's stretched-out body was lying there on the ground. "Run, Mary, run!" Mary Pat didn't bother to look. She just got up and ran as fast as she could toward the fence that separated their house from the orchard.

Not looking back, she ran until she reached the barbed-wire fence and dove quickly over it, distanced from the cow, the field, the apple trees, her brother, and the boy that navigated her run. She shivered, remembering the feel of the grounds vibration from hooves galloping toward her. Over the barbed wire she went—her blue jeans caught on one of the barbs and ripped an exact *L*-shaped tear in the leg of her jeans. As she caught her breath and regrouped at the edge of the fence, staring at her blue jeans—the boys off in the distance quiet now just watching to be sure she was okay—it all came flooding back.

She had dreamed this the night before, and now it was happening! The apple orchard, the boys riding and stirring up the cows, her mother's call to her, the fall, her race to the fence, and the perfect *L*-shaped rip in her jeans—all of it—she had already experienced in her dream. How could that be? Brian's voice, "Run, Mary, run!" etched in her soul. She dashed toward home, now safely on the other side, answering her mother's demanding call, puzzled that she had already lived this moment in a dream.

He couldn't be gone. Was that really possible that Brian wasn't coming home from Vietnam alive?

Wasn't he always there—there when Mary Pat was in the foster home due to the abuse in her house? It was Brian, her friend, who drove the ninety-mile round-trip to visit her. It wasn't her family—not her sisters or brothers or even her mother; it was Brian.

What was Brian's connection to her then? He had a girlfriend, and Mary Pat was still too young to be a real girlfriend! Though she was beginning to see him in a different light. After all, he was adorable to look at. But he was her brother's friend, the boy who moved into town and all the girls liked. But here he was; he came to see her. He reminded her that she would be okay, that she could handle whatever she needed to, even this. Even having to move to a strange town, living in a stranger's home, going to a different school, and not knowing anyone—but the reality was, the abuse would be over now. She could handle this. That was the main thing, so he reminded her that whatever it was that she had to experience in this new unfamiliar place, she could handle it and she would be okay. The reassurance helped her do just that—though terribly hurt, angry, lonely, and confused about life, she handled the foster home and the isolation she felt.

Sometimes—a lot of times—her pain expressed itself in rebellion against herself. It was Brian who calmed her rage and fear. He gave her a reprieve from all the unfamiliar around her by bringing a safe face that she knew and had come to love. He was a refuge in her storm of life, even as a young abused little teenage girl. It was Brian who was her soft place to fall. She found solace in his face, his laugh, his chuckle, his sincere care for her. He was like medicine to her soul, just by being him.

On his visit to the foster home, he took Mary Pat rowing in a boat. They found a local pond in the plush beautiful mountains of Pennsylvania. The day was like magic. The sun reflected from the rippling water, making a glimmering light penetrating through every fear of the child's life. Who was this young man, who made it all okay, who made life make some sort of sense, who brought an innocence into a young girl's marred, hurting soul? Brian rowed. Mary Pat gleaned the joy. They laughed and laughed and laughed the day away until it was time to say good-bye, and he would return to the familiar little hometown, and she, to a world of unfamiliar faces. It was as if he knew and had given her what she needed to face it all head-on. He represented all good, all comfort and kindness to her. Yes, she loved him. It was Brian who showed her what love was meant to be. His calm manner sustained her once again. As months passed and time moved forward, Mary Pat accepted a new home, a new place, a new family. During that time, she had a dream.

Its vividness never left her. She saw each detail of the dream acutely. She woke from the dream with a sense of dreaded darkness. It was haunting to her, yet it was just a dream. During gym class that day, she could hardly stay focused on the exercise, her mind troubled over what she saw in her dream.

She was crouched down in a hole in the ground with dirt walls around her. The hole was no more than three feet deep and two feet wide. There was a bamboo crate with a crisscross pattern over her head, covering the hole. The openings between the pattern allowed her to breathe, though imprisoned in this hole. There were people staring down at her, but they weren't American people. Their eyes were different, small, dark, round, staring, threatening to her. She knew she was a prisoner here somehow, and they held her captive. Then, in her dream, it was no longer her in that hole. She wasn't sure who it was. She couldn't see them, but she felt as if she was looking through their eyes and seeing what they could see from the hole they were in. She knew these people were going to kill the person in the hole. She was looking at them through the eyes of the captured. The next thing she saw in her dream, she had been transported to a room where there was a coffin in a funeral home setting. There were two rose-lit scone lamps on each end of the coffin, and flowers—flowers, vivid-colored flowers, multicolored flowers—surrounded the area near the coffin, and a glowing rose-color light cast a pink aura on the walls behind the coffin. Then she woke up. The dream was over. Its image tormented her and the death of it too real for dreams.

Three years and a Vietnam War later, she saw the very dream before her eyes when she walked into the funeral parlor where Brian lay under a glass that sealed him in his coffin. How was she to know? She was in that hole with him. She saw through his eyes; she felt what the person in the hole felt. Was it Brian?

She will never know, but the scene in the dream of the coffin and the funeral parlor was Brian's. And she knew the dread of the loss long before she knew it would be Brian that she would lose.

When Brian was a senior in high school, he knew he wanted to join the Army after graduation, and that's what he did. He completed his basic training and went on in Fort Benning, Georgia, to become a paratrooper. His letter was filled with the excitement he felt from his first jump! He absolutely marveled over the experience of jumping from an airplane with a parachute for security! The awe he expressed in his letter was contagious. She was sure nothing ever compared to the rush he felt falling through the sky until that cord was pulled and that chute opened! He was ecstatic over it, and the joy he felt poured out in the words of his letters. Brian was happy; he was doing what he wanted to do. He was training to serve. It was during this time of his life that he wanted Mary Pat to know he loved her. She wasn't just his best friend's little sister anymore. Before joining the Army, when he was still a senior, he wrote letters and sent cards and expressions of how he felt about her. He would love her "forever and always." But then Vietnam would steal him. His happiness changed to horror. What he had to do and be in Vietnam started taking a toll on his innocence, and Mary Pat felt him drifting farther away from himself and her.

CHAPTER 2

THERE WAS AN URGENCY IN my mother's pace; there always was. We rushed hand in hand down Franklin Avenue. The race into the center of town, off the big hill, tired my little legs as I tried to keep up with my mother's hurried steps. The smell of kerosene lingered in my nostrils. Mom had just finished dousing my head in kerosene to rid my hair of head lice. My scalp burned, and though Mom washed the kerosene out of my hair, the odor clung to me heavy, even out here in the open air around me. I was four years old; it was 1957. I was unaware and too young to know that I was about to have my first experience with social class difference in America. Mom hurried me along as I chattered incessantly about this and that and this and anything my little being could conjure up. I loved talking. I was fascinated by letters and words at an early age and used to tell my brother Gandy that "we must be special because we had words and animals didn't, they had to use sounds." Our sounds made words, and that intrigued me. Still, walking off that hill, Mom kept demanding that I be quiet. Somehow that did not compute. I kept talking, until finally I realized the anger in her voice. She seriously meant for me to shut up. So I did, at least for a while. All the time in the silence, my mind was talking to me, *Wonder where we are going? Wonder why we have to go so fast? How come we are always hurrying? Where is Gandy?*

My mind kept triggering one question after another, until I finally verbalized, "Mom, where are we going?"

"We are going to get our surplus," she responded impatiently.

"What is surplus, Mom?"

"Oh, Mary Pat, can you just be quiet for once?"

She sounded like my talking was painful, so I was quiet—for as long as I could be, without too much bother—until suddenly my thoughts began to explore where my brother Gandy might be. I thought about the nuns over at Saint John's School where Gandy attended with the teachers who wore long black robes and head-dresses that were sort of scary. I recalled how we would get cookies from them if we stopped at the kitchen door of the house they lived in called "the convent." We could get "holy cards" too. Although I didn't really know what they were, I savored the washed antique colors of the robes and the beautiful faces of the "saints," of even Jesus Himself! I collected as many cards as I could. I was proud of having them, especially because my Aunt Trese had some too, carefully placed here and there near pictures in her home. I knew having these cards must be close to having what you needed in life! The nuns were called Catholics. I guess Gandy was called a Catholic too, 'cause he went to school there. I would be a Catholic too, 'cause I would go there when I got big enough. Besides, Aunt Trese—who was my father's sister—made my mother send Gandy and me to Catholic school because it seems she was convinced we were going to "hell" if we weren't raised Catholic. I was more interested in what they said rather than in what they were called. Gandy had a catechism. It was a book he learned his school lessons from. I could recite that book verbatim and taught Gandy, even though he was older than me, 'cause I liked the words and he didn't.

"Who made you?"

"God made me."

"Why did God make you?"

"God made me to show His goodness and make me happy with Him in heaven."

I had no idea about the reality or the disillusion of all that, but it made me wonder about things—especially as I journeyed speech-less down that steep hill, racing with my mother's hand in mine drag-ging me along—like, if God made the first man, Adam, and the first woman, Eve, and He made me and I had a belly button, then did Adam and Eve have belly buttons?

So out of what seemed like the blue to my mother, I asked, "Mom, did Adam and Eve have belly buttons?"

Aghast, she said, "Mary Pat, you stop that nonsense right now! You be quiet and quit asking foolish questions all the time," like we would be struck dead by the God that made us if I asked or even talked about the idea of a belly button!

"Yes, ma'am."

An uneasy space of silence, my mind in deep thought, still reasoning, we hurried along. I was bent on the idea that if God made everything like those nuns said, then He was responsible for me having head lice, 'cause He made them, and that just didn't seem like a very nice thing to me. Of course, I would have questions! Who wouldn't? The remainder of the race down the hill, I pouted. I thought about a lot of things—Mr. Castro's flowers, how beautiful his garden was (how could there be so many different kinds of flowers in one garden?), Mrs. Pangerelli's big beautiful red house—and thought how nice it was of her to throw her clothes out on the ash pile so we could get them. They never had worn or frayed threads; they were never stained or old. She could have given them to the Goodwill or the Salvation Army, but instead, she would put them in boxes at the ash pile near our house, and she never said anything when she would see us carry the boxes home. She would just close her curtains like she didn't need the sun shining in anymore. And when we wore the clothes, she would just act like she never saw them and say, "Oh, Mary Pat, don't you look just lovely today? My, that color suits you just fine."

We kept walking. We passed Mr. Saleacho and his dog, Sammy. What a good friend Sammy was to Mr. Saleacho, who didn't have anyone to love but that dog. At the bottom of the hill, we raced by a fence that held rows and rows of tomato vines tied on stakes— plump, red tomatoes.

A strong voice called out, "Dorothy, if you want any of these tomatoes, you just stop and pick what you need now for you and those young'uns a' yours."

"Thank you very much, Mr. Gonamassi. I will remember that," she said as we raced right past the big gate.

17

Yeah, maybe if there was a God, He wasn't so bad after all. A lot of nice was all around me. My pouting anger went away, and I decided, if there was a God, what a good idea.

We reached the side street and climbed a few shabby gray wooden steps that were in obvious need of paint. Mom opened the big door that squeaked on its old, rusted hinges. I followed in silence. Inside I stood frozen, studying everything this side of that door. The air was pungent, people presented worn, their faces creased by what appeared to be defeat. Dullness possessed the room and its occupants. The inside appeared dark compared to the bright sunshine of natural lighting we were leaving behind us. Soon after we entered the narrow room, my eyes started adjusting to the lack of light and to the shadows made by the bare lightbulbs that hung like stark bells sporadically from the ceiling.

This place is creepy, I thought, still not talking. *And it stinks too, and it's not my kerosene head either, it's something else.*

People were gathered in lines, single file, one behind the other. Mom and I joined the end of a line.

"Mom, is this surplus? What is surplus?"

Mom ignored me, as if I hadn't said anything. She didn't even tell me to be quiet; she just acted as if she wasn't there, as if I wasn't there either. She stood staring in the line with all the others. They were standing face-to-back waiting, face-to-back waiting, one soul after another, single file, face-to-back. No one was talking; no conversations were taking place. No words. Silence and shuffling and dread all around me.

What are we doing here? I thought to myself, *I wish Gandy was here, and Becca and Sarra and Benn, all my brothers and sisters.* I didn't want to be alone here with Mom. *How come I had to be here with her? How come she had to be here anyway?*

But she couldn't hear me; she just stared, blank-faced, looking right through me, as if I wasn't there.

At the front of the narrow room, there was a long table and a big desk with a sharp-nosed woman whose colors were much brighter than any of the colors in line. She was the only one who said any words. There was no kindness in her voice or in her tone. She was busy with paperwork and sternness.

I don't like her, I thought to myself. I wasn't sure why I didn't like her. I was trying to figure that out when I heard her call another name without expression or care, just monotone.

"Mr. Sabin."

I felt some kind of guilt for not liking her. *After all, what did she do to me?* She glared at us. I glared back and made a face, scrunching up my nose at her. *I hope Mom didn't see that.* I guess I didn't have to worry about that. Whatever happened to Mom after we got in this room made her seem far away.

Meanwhile, Ms. Stern Face continued to call out names, "Joseph Smith. Bob Blaise. Mrs. Tracey."

I held my mother's hand tightly the closer we got to the big desk and the woman sitting at it. Her clothes were vivid in color. Our clothes were dull, more worn, more dated, no frills. She seemed to notice that too. She treated us different, different than the way our nice neighbors did or the nice people we saw as we walked urgently to this place—this dark place. As my four-year-old mind absorbed the scene around me, this scene that I was part of, time stopped for me. I looked around, and it was as if everything had frozen in time. Nothing moved, no one moved—no sounds, no shuffling, no sighing—as if we were all statues carved in time. At that second, I realized how truly different we were in that room from everyone outside of that room. Coming through that door separated us from other people who never had to walk through that door and stand in this line, under the scrutiny of a woman who observed us as unworthy of her words. Coming through that door differentiated us—not just for this moment in time, but for days long after we would leave and then again have to return to this room, to this line, to this surplus. I looked at those around me, the dullness of our being intensified for me. I saw burdens in the wrinkles of faces, worn by time and troubles. I looked at myself and my clothes: missing a button, shoes scuffed, hair that residually smelled of kerosene. I looked like everyone else in this room, and until that moment in time, I had no idea I was any different than anyone else on our street. My friends, Christine and

Mickey, never told me I was. They never made me feel like I wasn't like them. Even when they had pennies for chocolate and I didn't, they shared and never said a word. Now, here in this stark atmosphere, in front of this condescending woman, I now realized why Mom and I were in this line for surplus, for food to feed the "poor."

I am poor. We are poor. That second of time, was it God?

Life went from animation to still frame. I realized I was right where I belonged.

There was something bigger than me that allowed me to be here for a purpose—something that allowed a four-year-old child to understand what being poor felt like and how deeply it hurts one's soul to be labeled different from others. I was right where I belonged. The unspoken desperation of the poor filled my soul. I was changed. Time started again, the rustling of the brown paper bags rescinded.

"Dorothy Avery," echoed from the lips of the woman at the desk.

My mother stepped forward. We filled our bags with peanut butter, flour, powdered milk, powdered eggs, and blocks of cheese. Only the sighs of a woman already exhausted by life could be heard through the rustling of the brown paper sacks, as we filled ours.

My mother—I knew now why her steps were so urgent, why her pace always so desperate, why her heart so vocally still, why her eyes so distantly sad, and why her emotions to me always seemed to be detached. My mother was going to have a "quiet walk" back up the hill of Franklin Avenue, going home with Mary Pat silently by her side. To be an adult and be poor carried a much heavier sorrow than being four and poor. I understood. Silence flooded her soul. I learned.

"There was a time to speak and a time to be silent, a time to every purpose under heaven" (Ecclesiastes, KJV).

CHAPTER 3

I WAS BORN ON A chilly November 10 night in 1953. Dad never married Mom. He had been married prior to his relationship with my mother, and as I understood it, his Catholic faith wouldn't allow or acknowledge a remarriage to my mother. So my brother Gandy and I were born as what other kids called bastards. That was always a little confusing to me as a child as I didn't really know what a bastard was; I just knew it didn't feel like something good. Now today it appears having a child prior to marriage is all the go. Morals have shifted, and marriage is being threatened and redefined and under scrutiny as if a man marrying a woman was the wrong thing to do. Who would have thought that back in the '50s?

Well, anyway, it takes my mother to tell the story of the night I was born. I'll try to do her story justice.

Dorothy had not seen a doctor her entire pregnancy while carrying me. I am not sure why prior to the fifth month, she never went to the doctor, but I can tell you why after the fifth month she never went. Stubbornness, plain foolish stubbornness—because she decided that after my father, who was an alcoholic, didn't show up as he was supposed to in order to pay for a doctor's visit in her fifth month of pregnancy, she was determined *not* to go to a doctor at all after that! He was guilty, and she was going to show him!

He wanted her to go, she said, and she refused to, saying, "Serves him right for not being there when he was supposed to be!"

It obviously never dawned on her that it was for her own good, and possibly mine! Somehow she thought this punishment of guilt and shame was more important. Regardless, when it came time for delivery, the baby would be born at home. So I was. She said that made Dad nervous too. I guess so, because the story has it he was nowhere around. He was stuck again in the local gin mill, having "just one more" drink—which Mom was certain he would be doing, nervous or not. The rest of the story struck me when I heard it because I picture this woman alone in the chill of a November Pennsylvania night birthing her baby, out of her own stubbornness or need not to bow to some alcoholic man who let her down "again."

She descended to the cellar in anticipation of a delivery that night, to fill the furnace with wood and stoke the fire for embers, which would burn for her late into the night when she would be in the throes of birthing and unable to tend to the furnace. She called for a Christian neighbor lady who was always there if Mom wanted her. As I aged, I recall the significance I felt that the first woman to hold me loved Jesus, in spite of the fact that I was born out of stubbornness that night! Mom said that she always felt guilty that my eyes were weak all my life; she thought it was her fault because my eyes weren't washed out with "whatever they wash a newborn's eyes out with." She was certain that affected my vision. I never thought it was that simple. She also said, while sharing my birthing story with me, that she felt guilty because she knew she didn't eat right while carrying me, because she said that what little food we had, she felt the other children needed it and felt bad taking it when there wasn't enough for them. She "didn't want to be taking food out of their mouths"—that's how she said it—when she "knew they were hungry and needed it."

Mom had four other children at the time, little ones to feed: Benn, Sarra, Becca, and Gandy. Mom's first babies, David and Donald, died when they were infants. But our brother Richie died when he was nine years old. He drowned in the Susquehanna River. He left our family before that chilly November night that I was born.

Another brother, Tommy, left our family before we ever got to see him. Mom adopted him out. Unlike me, he was born in a hospital. Now, looking back, it was probably part of the plan. Mom had Merlin in her life, and there was no room for the kids she already had as far as he was concerned—let alone adding a new baby to the clan. Whoever the father was to my new little brother, I found out that my mother and her new man were going to have nothing to do with raising him. The hospital helped adopt him out.

Becca walked into the room. "Mary Pat, what are you doing with your apron way up there?"

Becca was babysitting me, and I was playing "house," my apron pulled high up around my chest.

"That isn't how you wear an apron!"

Defiantly responding, I said, "Yes, it is! It's where Mommy wears hers!"

"Yeah, but Mommy is going to have a baby, and you're not, so fix your apron!"

I stood stunned, trying to decipher the words of my sister as she tugged at my makeshift apron and tied it at my waistline.

"Is Mommy really going to have a baby? Are we getting a new baby?"

I was delighted at the thought of it, although another part of me felt embarrassed that I didn't know the right way to wear an apron. A new baby was coming to live with us! No other words were ever spoken about it, and my mother continued to wear her apron below her breasts, high on her chest, covering her big belly.

Then one night—while Becca was sitting with me in our living room playing our vinyl records and singing the country songs that always made me feel like I could cry but never did—Becca said, "Mommy won't be coming home tonight. She has gone to the hospital to have the baby." A long pause, then she said, "Mary Pat, the baby won't be coming home with her."

"Not coming home? What, Becca? What do you mean? Why? I thought we were getting a new baby?"

Fear gripped me. What could this mean, after all this time of waiting for our new baby? Why wasn't the baby coming home?

"How could this be? I had prepared my heart for this new little one ever since the time I learned the right way to wear an apron. Where is our baby going?" I pleaded.

"Mary Pat, the baby is a little boy. They named him Tommy. He will go to live with another family that wants him. At the hospital, Dr. Davis has made the arrangement with Mom. That's called adoption. Tommy will be adopted and go to a different home than ours."

"Yeah, but we want him to come here and live with us! He is our baby, not theirs!" I said, and I was mad and crushed 'cause Tommy never did come home.

After that day, it was never discussed. I was instructed to "be quiet" about it. I stuffed him in my heart with all the other things we could never talk about. Nothing of importance was ever talked about—that's how it seemed to me. Everything was a secret, or an order to keep silent about, including the domestic abuse and child molestation that followed with the new man in the house.

Sarra went to school after Tommy's birth and confessed, "I didn't know what to say about our new baby."

Her friend's mother was carrying a child the same time as Mom. Her friend came to school with pictures and boasting of love and pride for her new baby brother. Sarra felt guilty and cheated all at the same time.

She didn't know what to say or how to explain we had no new baby brother that came home. Sarra later said through pursed lips, "He was lucky to have been given away. He missed the abuse in our house."

I'm not sure. I guess he is where he is supposed to be. But we still missed knowing our baby brother.

CHAPTER 4

THE BRIDGE WAS CROWDED WITH onlookers peering over the edge, down into the dark water of the night. The powerful search-lights pierced the river, causing rays to penetrate the deepness of the dark water. In the beacon, particles of mud and debris vibrated through the light of each ray.

Over the humming of the generators, you could hear the emergency workers' urgent commands, "Lift the line, we need to go further up! Loosen the coil, we need some slack."

While the townspeople were gathered, huddled in curiosity and dread, on the bridge arched over the river and its workers below, somewhere in the rivers depth of the murky water was little Richie. It had been hours since he left to go to the river to get sand for his turtle. He never returned.

The Susquehanna River ran directly behind the apartment where Dorothy lived with Benn, Richie, Becca, Sarra, and Gandy. The boys always played there—throwing rocks in the river, swimming, fishing, gathering crawdads, or bringing home turtles and minnows. Benn was the oldest of the boys, and he went with Richie to the river. It was early afternoon. The boys hadn't been gone long when Benn came running in, calling, "Mom, hurry, I can't find Richie. I can't find him, Mom. Hurry!"

Tippy, the boys' dog, seemed to understand the urgency and beckoned, coaxing as well for Dorothy to come. Tippy was barking and barking, wagging, zigging and zagging motion, running ahead, looking behind to ensure that Dorothy was following the right path to the river's edge.

Dorothy, rushing to the river, yelled out, "Riiiichieeee! Riiiicheeee! Richie, where are you? Richie, answer me! Richie please, please, where are you?"

Dorothy continued to call frantically for her son as Benn too hollered loudly for our brother. Tippy ran to a spot at the water's edge and stood barking nonstop, nose directed to the last place Benn reported seeing Richie. After the initial panic and desperation of the moment, not finding her son, Dorothy returned to call for help. The rescue workers dragged the river the whole afternoon into the night.

Dorothy told the children, "Now, you stay here, and don't go out. I'm going down to the bridge, and you mustn't come there or go anywhere. Stay put in this house. I will be back."

Becca and Sarra put a crate up to the window of the second-story apartment, and together they stood, watching from the distance at the rays in the night coming from near the bridge where the search continued for their little brother.

"Do you feel sad?" Becca asked Sarra as they stood together, peeking out the window.

"Yes, do you?" replied Sarra.

"I feel mad!" said Becca. "How come that happened to our brother, huh? How come? He was a nice brother! He never hit us!"

"I know," said Sarra, breaking down and crying.

"Don't cry, don't cry, Sarra. They will find him."

"But what if they don't, what if he never comes home?"

"Don't worry, he will come home, they will find him."

Together the two little girls comforted each other, standing on the crate, noses to the window, waiting for Richie. On the bridge, curious passersby and caring townsfolk continued to wait as the river was dragged for Richie's body. The searchlights pierced the darkness, and the generator's grind went long into the night. Dorothy hid in the shadow of the bridge, waiting with anxiety and fear, unable to comprehend the truth of the moment and what was really happening. Was this all real? Would she wake up and Richie be home with her and her other children?

In the murmurs from the crowd, she heard the judgment of those unaware of her presence in the shadows where she stood on the bridge.

"That woman has so many kids she can't keep track of them."

"Why would she ever let those boys go down to that river, anyway? There is no way that boy is alive."

Dorothy's heart wanted to explode, but instead, she stared into the river into the night, waiting for Richie.

Later after the midnight hour, Richie was found—his little blue body shriveled with the water's saturation.

Dorothy doesn't recall much after that. She identified her son, and the wrinkles of his skin haunted her.

Richie was laid out in the living room of Dorothy's apartment. The school children came by grades to view his body—Benn's grade, then Becca's grade, then Sarra's grade—one child after another climbing the second-story stairs and parading past the coffin that held their classmate. Sarra, Becca, and Benn sat quietly in steel folding chairs near their dead brother in the starkness of the apartment.

Gandy sat on Dorothy's lap. He was a baby and wasn't fully aware of what death had just done to Richie.

Dorothy was poor, and there were no luxuries—no dainties, no pleasant rugs, nor lamps—to welcome the children and parents that came to pay their respects. The coffin was set like a piece of out-of-place furniture in the living room. That night after the viewers and the fourth and fifth grade classes left, Benn stood alone in the room with his dead little brother, gripped by guilt that he didn't save him. Benn stood, waiting, hoping that somehow Richie was still going to be alive, hoping that tomorrow Richie would walk home from the river with the excitement of a can of sand and some river bugs to feed their turtles.

But reality was, Richie wasn't coming home, and Benn carried shame and guilt after that—which affected his whole life's journey. The family lived, but they survived under a cloud of tragedy and deep loss.

The living room was silent as the little ones paraded by viewing their dead friend, haunted by the shushed fearful whispers of scared parents: "You must never play by the river."

Richie and Becca were in the same classroom at school and had the same classmates. It was clear that Becca changed from grieving Richie's loss. Becca held a deep heartache that was unable to heal from the loss of her brother. It hurt her heart to see his empty desk at school, and it all only made her feel angrier. Becca loved Richie. Even later, many years after Richie's drowning, when Becca became an adult, she was the one who bought Richie a headstone for his grave. She replaced the flat gray river stone, which was all her family could leave to mark his grave, with a real engraved headstone.

A few days after Richie's burial, Dorothy returned to the Susquehanna River to the place where Tippy barked and barked, returning to the spot that Richie was last reported being seen alive.

In her own words, Dorothy told me, "I felt like I couldn't go on. I had no ability to get up each day and face the world. I didn't want to live. I felt like I completely broke down. I walked to the river, and I was going to go in and just drown, like he did. But with those thoughts, as I entered the water, I heard his voice. I heard Richie's voice. I heard him as clear as if I was talking here with you. He said, 'I'm okay, Mom. Stay, Gandy needs you.'"

Dorothy left the river that day and lived for Gandy. She lived for him 'til her dying day.

Years after Richie's drowning and my addition to her life and my siblings' lives, Mom would be in the big attic at Franklin Avenue, packing winter clothes away and getting out the box of summer clothes that smelled of mothballs, with me by her side. She would take a small plastic zipped bag—stored in a little box, separated from everything else—and open it, holding the soft-textured striped shirt and cotton shorts against our cheeks; and the trace of a child and a brother I never knew was impressed upon me. The bag held a set of clothes that belonged to Richie. When I was old enough to understand what happened, she stopped taking me to the attic with her. She was too silent to expose her feelings, and if she had known that

I was not your typical child, I am certain she would never have held Richie's clothes in my presence.

It would have exposed her heart, and she learned long ago not to ever let her heart stay soft and open.

CHAPTER 5

LIFE DID GO ON AFTER Richie's death, but the repercussion of such a loss stayed etched in the dynamic of the family—every soul affected in its own way. They remained poor. They still gathered coal along the railroad tracks to put in their heating stove. They still wore hand-me-downs. They still were the family that was talked about in town—the only difference, Richie was gone. With his absence, Sarra moved up into taking over Richie's chores.

One day, after Sarra peeled potatoes, she mopped up the kitchen floor. She had a basin of dirty water with some of her potato peels floating on the surface. This caused a dilemma for Sarra.

She stood, thinking, *If I dump the water in the bath tub, I'll clog the tub. If I dump the water in the sink, I'll clog the drain. If I dump the water in the toilet, the toilet will back up.*

She got a genius idea that she knew would keep her out of trouble with Dorothy. She decided to dump the dirty water, potato peels and all, through a knothole in the floor of their apartment—except to Sarra's shock, the filthy water with its potato peels ended up landing right in the bed of the woman who lived below!

All heck broke loose! Sarra had some explaining to do when the neighbor came pounding on the door!

After the initial explosion of emotion, an explanation given, and all the "reasoning" behind Sarra's decision brought to light—everyone got a laugh out of it: Dorothy, Sarra, and even the neighbor whose bed was soaked with potato peels and dirty wash water! It was an unseen catharsis. The first time since Richie was gone, there was laughter in their house—a bit of guilt decomposed.

Soon after, the family moved to Washington Street in the nearby town of Susquehanna. Dorothy's mother lived there, and it was comforting to move away and start again. So Benn, Becca, Sarra, and Gandy moved with Dorothy. They now had a new neighbor—Old Mrs. Kanice—who didn't miss a trick in the new family's coming and going!

When Becca and Sarra would be out on their sidewalk, fastening their tin cans with rope around their feet to create makeshift stilts and clacking sounds when they walked, Mrs. Kanice would be peering at them through her window. When Benn would be out setting boxes up with string and sticks to "catch a bird," Mrs. Kanice would be peering out her window. When the little girls would share the steel roller skates with the precious key Sarra kept on a string around her neck, Mrs. Kanice would be peering out her window.

Most times she hid, and you could catch her nose through the curtains to "see what those kids were up to." Why, she had heard of them and that mother of theirs! Word traveled fast when a boy died, and here was that sinful mother and those kids of hers that she didn't take care of, and now no telling what they were up to!

Life carried on. Mom was mostly silent, except if she wanted to yell at you for something. She never talked about her past; she wouldn't even tell us who her father was.

Once, I came right out and asked, "Mom, who was your father?"

Her reply was simply, "You wouldn't want to know, he was a drunk."

But what she didn't realize was that I really did want to know, and so did the other kids. But we were never important enough to know, or be told by Dorothy, who our grandfather—her father—was. It was one of her hidden secrets. We were never allowed to cross that line of her secrets, and she had a lot of them.

We moved from the house on Washington Street to the black house on Church Street, to the green house at 503 Franklin Avenue. Grandfather Kelly, my father's father, helped my mother buy that house.

He gave the owner the thousand dollars down payment for Dorothy. I still frequented the convent across town on Church Street and got my free cookies and even candy and holy cards if I answered the catechism questions correctly! I had a beautiful collection of those cards! I found them fascinating and still today appreciate their awesome shades of color. I liked them a lot, but I never did know their meaning or purpose. Somehow they were too far from my family's reality to make any difference one way or another in my life. But I could appreciate the art of them. Plus, again, I did know my Aunt Trese was proud of my holy cards. I liked the attention over them. I'm not sure what difference they made to her either, but she collected them too and was glad I "properly collected them."

Aunt Trese and her family lived in my grandfather's home—a beautiful Victorian house with meticulous landscaping and red plush carpeting, which draped the handsome oak stairway ascending to a fairy-tale realm of beauty inside. Through my eyes, Grandfather's rooms were what all homes should look like—beds of oak and brass, mahogany wardrobes, down comforters, lace, wallpaper, and sweet odors easily breathed.

The closets were filled with clothes that actually fit the person they were intended for. They weren't hand-me-downs or too big or too tight or too short, and I wished I knew what that felt like. The bathroom in Grandfather's house was so big you could have placed another great room right in the middle of it and still had room! The bathtub had four clawed legs that lifted if off the black-and-white checkered floor. The sink was a matching pedestal with curves that made it look like a big flower in bloom to me! It was a beautiful house, and it truly smelled of order and richness—a stark contrast of our house and my mother's roots.

Quite in contrast, my maternal grandmother's house stunk. It was dirty, had bare lightbulbs hanging from the ceiling, and you could smell the bathroom in the hallway—even before you got into the bathroom—because they flushed the toilet with a bucket of water kept by the sink. I decided very young I wasn't going to have any bare lightbulbs or buckets of water to flush in my house; they were too intrusive. And my house was going to be clean and smell pretty!

The idea that Mom came from the poor and Dad came from "the other side of the tracks" might be why it appeared to me that my aunt never really liked my mother. She always treated her as if she were a servant, rather than the mother of her own flesh-and-blood niece and nephew.

One day, through laughter, Aunt Trese told the story of how she had seen Mom going across the lawn and thought it was her cleaning lady.

"Why, come to find out it was Dorothy, carrying her brown paper bags!"

My, my! What children's eyes see and hear!

Grandfather lived in one room of his house, in the room across from the big bathroom, right at the top of the stairs. As he aged, the climb became harder and harder. He stopped being able to drive his new Mercury cars, and so he lived in his home cared for and driven around as needed by his family who lived in his home with him. When I would go to visit Grandfather, Dad and I would climb the stairs and sit in his big chair by the window, the spot where Grandfather would sit for hours, reminiscing his life before old age came to call and take his memory.

I was reminded, "Don't touch the walls," as I climbed the staircase; I would "get them dirty." Embarrassed, I made sure I never did again, after the reminder.

I thought, *No matter what, I would learn how to be like Aunt Trese and her family—not like our family, poor and ignorant with an alcoholic for a father.*

Why, even my cousin reminded me once when I was visiting Grandfather, as we played on the playground with the other kids, that my father "wasn't worth one penny." I ran back to Grandfather's house and cried. Aunt Trese wanted to pick me up, asking what was wrong, but I wouldn't tell her, and I wouldn't let her hold me either. And somewhere deep within me, I thought, if being rich made you talk like that, I liked poor people better. I was in a dilemma, whether I wanted to be poor or rich. I decided it was a lot for a five-year-old to figure out. I started feeling "less than" at my visits. I am sure they never meant for me to feel that way, but they never stood in a surplus line, getting government cheese and powdered milk. They ate and drank the real stuff. They couldn't know what it really felt like being from the other side of the tracks, having people judge your mother and father, saying unkind things about either one of them. But through a child's eyes, not much reality is missed. A child knows and can read a heart.

Grandfather smoked a pipe, and it was apparent that Aunt Trese cringed over the smell of that pipe as much as she cringed when she saw my father coming to their house. On one of these perfectly sunny days, which was a perfect reason for Dad to start drinking, he and I walked hand in hand to visit Grandfather. We stopped by the big swing set at the park, and as Dad pushed me in the swing, I sang, "Oh to go up in an air-o-plane, sailing, sailing, sailing so high … Oh, to go up in an air-o-plane, sailing into the sky." Oh my, what fun! No worries! Just pure fun swinging in the open air with my dad pushing me in the swing! What joy!

When we left the playground and got to Grandfather's house, we walked up to the big wraparound porch and knocked on the oversized door. Aunt Trese appeared, leaving the screen door closed between her and us. She didn't invite us in. Instead, she called for Grandfather. Leaving us waiting by the door, she departed. We stood waiting until it was obvious that we weren't going upstairs to see Grandfather; he was coming down to us. So realizing he would be needing time to descend the stairs, Dad and I sat on the top step of the stairs leading to the porch, waiting for Grandfather to appear. As I sat there, I started worrying, *Had I touched the walls and got them dirty, is that why we couldn't go in and see Grandfather? Did I forget and do something that poor people do, embarrassing my dad and me now and preventing us from being able to go up into Grandfather's room?*

After accumulated worried minutes of waiting, Grandfather appeared at the screen. Dad and I jumped up, expecting to enter his home and visit. Instead, Grandfather chided, "Francis, I told you to never come here when you've been drinking." And he closed the door. That was it … That was all. Dad did not offer a word of rebuttal. He just took my hand; we sat back down on the top step of the porch. He had a sad look in his eyes.

"Puddin' head, how 'bout you and me go back to the big swing?"

My heart broke. I not only saw the pain of rejection in my father's eyes. I felt the rejection in my own as well. Not wasting a minute to fix the situation, I patted my father's leg with my pudgy little fingers, "It's okay, Daddy, you can come here anytime you want," as if my patting would make the hurt go away, his and mine.

The swing didn't feel the same after that, and I don't know what we did for the rest of our time that day; but I do know, subconsciously, my trust for pretty places and the pretty people in them changed. Years later, in the public records at the county seat, I saw that my father had signed his part of Grandfather's house over for one dollar to Aunt Trese and Uncle Nunzio. Alcohol is no good for a man's sense of worth.

CHAPTER 6

IT WAS FUN WALKING TO Saint John's School from across town, down the big hill of Franklin Avenue and through Main Street up the hill to Broad Avenue, where the redbrick school towered high above the surrounding houses. Gandy and I had many nice walks together in all kinds of weather, and I grew to cherish those walks and the change of seasons. I loved the birds we saw as we walked and the clear blue skies with its puffy clouds at times. I loved the smell of the autumn air and the sound of the rustling of the fallen leaves beneath our feet. I loved the rain tapping against our skin and the freshness of wind brushing our faces. I loved the snow and the patterns it made in the landscape. I loved the sound of the creek in the spring when the water rushed to the river. I loved it all, and I especially loved walking with my brother Gandy. He always felt like my little brother even though he was older than I was. It seemed as if I had to protect him somehow from all that wasn't good, because he was such a good kid. I learned easier than he did, so I taught him how to read better and taught him his catechism lessons. When we played "school," even though I was younger, I was always the teacher, not Gandy. He was just fine with that, and it just seemed like it was how it was supposed to be! He was the pupil; I was teacher. But it was Gandy who taught me how to fish and ride a bike and catch crawdads in the creek.

We tromped through the woods together and ate frog legs on wood fires he made by the water. Gandy was always a part of me, and our walks to and from school only enhanced our bond as sister and brother.

Sarra wasn't quite as loving. She seemed to have a mean streak toward me. She would pick on me and tell people that I was a "brat and was always throwing up." Mom would say, "Leave Mary Pat alone, she has a nervous stomach." I'm not sure how anyone lived in our house without one. And maybe I was a brat.

After all, I did get in trouble for telling Mickey what I learned about Santa Claus. And I did remember that time, I had "a good talking to" for telling Christine the difference between boys and girls! Sarra may have seen the brat in those bad doings. But I still liked Sarra. I thought she was interesting, with nice friends; they were always kind to me. I was happy that one of her friends' mothers would feed Sarra real food. It always made Sarra in a better mood, and then she treated me more kindly too. I knew it hurt Sarra that we were poor. She remembered opening our refrigerator and seeing nothing but a can of evaporated milk and a piece of cheese.

Once, Aunt Trese brought Christmas packages for Gandy and me, and Sarra stood and watched Aunt Trese take presents from the trunk of her car, but Sarra didn't get one. Sarra hated me for that. Gandy and I had a different father from all our siblings, but we had no control over that. It was rare for Aunt Trese to bring Gandy and me a gift, let alone bring anything to our siblings. But when you're a little kid and you see somebody else get something and you get left out, it pricks your heart and makes you mad. Sarra took her anger out on me. Becca was just the opposite. She clearly loved me. I didn't have to stay away from Becca, like Sarra told me to do. Becca wanted me with her. And typically, she took me everywhere with her. Even when she was angry or upset, it was never directed toward me; she was a safe place for me to be in the middle of the chaos of our lives. Becca was ten years older than me, and it was Becca who nurtured me and took care of me growing up. Why, Becca would even take me to the Sugar Bowl on Main Street, the hangout for the teens in that day.

The jukebox would be playing music, the air filled with tunes—"Soldier boy, oh, my little soldier boy, I'll be true to you," or "She wore blue velvet," or Elvis—the late 1950 early 1960 songs. The music mingled with the smell of vanilla taffy from the big red taffy machine Mrs. Zaharass had there. She would have taffy pulls for the teens, and the girls in their pony skirts and bobby socks would laugh and dance and the boys would roll their cigarettes up in the sleeve of their white tight T-shirts, laughing while they drank Coca-Cola from glass bottles and ate Wise potato chips. Becca included me in it all—innocent fun and some of my favorite memories as the little sister that tagged along with her big sister.

Benn wasn't as available as Becca but was a nice big brother. He always called me "little sister" and would do funny sounds, like Donald Duck, with his voice when he was trying to get me to laugh. Once, he said, "Ya know how to get your sleep and watch a movie at the same time?" Perplexed, I said, "No." He said, "You keep one eye open to watch the movie and sleep with the other eye closed!" He was always making up something silly. "Does a house burn 'up,' or does a house burn 'down'?" I would laugh, and he would tickle me then throw me up in the air, then off he would go. He was busy. He worked and made his own way. He fished and hunted and spent lots of time at the river. It was Benn who would put me on his shoulders to go hiking through the woods to get a tree at Christmas. My siblings were part of my gift.

And then there were the times that I would be with Mom, who seemed to be the "nurse" to the other poor families in town.

One day, Little Lester Calway showed up at our torn screen door, just a-bangin' and a-bangin' for all he was worth—all outta breath and huffin' from the race to our house.

"Mrs., Mrs., Mrs., Mrs., Momma said come quickly, Momma needs ya, Momma needs ya, please come now, Momma needs ya."

Mom seemed to know the need. She gathered herself, a white sheet, a can of tomato soup, a big bed spread, my book, and then took my hand, and we hustled out the door at the heels of Little Lester. Four houses and a good stretch down the hill, we entered Mrs. Calway's house. Mrs. Calway was not to be seen; she was in her bedroom off the living room. I received my strict orders: "Now, you sit right here, and don't you move."

Mom proceeded to take the big spread and covered the doorway to hide the bed where Mrs. Calway was lying. Murmuring and muffled voices came from behind the curtain-like door. Mom boiled hot water and took the white sheet with her behind the curtain. Groans and sounds that seemed like pain came from Mrs. Calway. I sat frozen as ordered, unable to do anything else. Whatever was happening behind that curtain, I was more than glad to be on this side of it! Little Lester sat robotic too, eyes widening at every pleading groan coming from the curtained room that Mrs. Calway and my mother occupied into the late afternoon hours. I was relieved Mom brought my *Woody Woodpecker* book with us. I read the words and showed the pictures over and over again to Little Lester, who seemed on the verge of tears any minute. During the waiting and pressing on, Mom opened the can of tomato soup, added water, and fed me and Little Lester. We sipped our soup hungrily and gratefully. We munched our soda crackers and drank our grape Kool-Aid without stirring a wink outside of Mrs. Calways' bedroom door. In time, we heard the cry—a burst of life—a newborn entered the world. An exhausted flood of relief ushered into the whole house. Lester cried.

He had a new baby sister, and his Momma was okay. His Momma was okay. He had a new baby sister.

Monday was washday. Mom washed our clothes in a big wash pot filled with steamy water atop the wood-cooking stove in the kitchen. I knew not to touch the pot or the silver handle that was used to remove the solid cast iron lid from the top of the big cast iron stove. Mom would get the pot of water boiling; rolling steam would bellow from the big kitchen kettle. Mom would push the clothes down into the scalding water with a wooden stick, which really was an old chair leg, stripped and worn smooth—just right for dipping and retrieving the wash from the big pot. The steam made droplets of water on our windows. No matter what, washday was Monday. If it rained or snowed, the clothes were hung on ropes inside, stretched throughout the house, to dry. If it was sunny or dry, the clothes were hung on the big clothesline outback by Tippy. Tippy, our big black furry friend, we all loved. He was tied out back and had his own doghouse that was positioned exactly right for an aerial view overlooking the town of Susquehanna. Below you could see the treetops, housetops, and the creek that ran between Front Street and our house on

Franklin Avenue. High on that hill holding my dog, Tippy, with the town and trees below us, I felt awe about life—almost like what you feel when you realize that the moon isn't just a light but really a whole ball suspended in space with nothing supporting it. That's how I felt outback, holding Tippy. I was sure life was good, even if we were hungry sometimes. The awe of life outweighed any hunger pains or humiliation of who we were to others or to ourselves.

Dad lived with us on Franklin Avenue. I was sure it was because it was Dad's father who helped Mom buy the house. Dad and Mom were in constant battle mode. Dad drank too much and too often.

Mom truly was exhausted trying to make life work for her and her kids. She lived furious over it all.

When Dad would come in from his work on the railroad, he'd be under the influence of alcohol. When he would get paid, he would spend his money drinking before Mom would have the chance to pay the utilities or get groceries. Typically, the ritual on payday was Mom gathering Gandy and me, and off we would go, racing to the pay window at the depot downtown. I always hoped Dad hadn't beat us to the beautiful wood-grain ornate window, with its massive wood-carved detail and steel bars separating the clerk and my mother. I hoped we weren't too late. I learned dread over the whole process.

It was scary when we would hear, "Mr. Kelly has picked up his pay, ma'am."

We came to understand what would follow: bills would not be paid; utilities would be shut off; groceries would be scarce; screaming, yelling, and fighting would fill the atmosphere of our home. Dad definitely did not meet the needs of our family, but I never feared him, even when he was drunk. He didn't hit me, and he was never mean to me. I came to learn he was antagonistic when he drank, but I still was never afraid of Dad. I had to age to realize what antagonistic really meant. He would come home drunk and crank up our old record player, blasting the country Western tunes. He would let me sit on his lap, and we would park in a chair right in front of the old phonograph, playing the vinyl records with the album cover of a dog singing into a megaphone.

He would crank the volume so high that Mom would come flying into the room in no time flat.

"For cramp's sake, Frank, turn that music down!" she said as she bitterly turned the volume down.

And then Dad would give me one of those surprise faces with big open eyes and a round-shaped *O* to his lips, wearing a "we're in big trouble" grin. Then right back up the volume would go, and his look changed to a "watch what happens now" look! And in would come Mom—a little steamier than before, a little louder than before—again, turning down the volume. Then Dad and I would giggle. She would turn it down; Dad would turn it up. She would turn it down; Dad would turn it up. I thought it was a game we all played together. It was the only time I recalled my mom, dad, and me doing anything together. Even though she was yelling, I thought it was part of the game. Dad and I were having fun. I had no idea it really wasn't fun for her!

I can still hear him whisper as he cranks the sound back up, "Okay, wait, here she comes, here she comes!"

Then he would give me that big surprised look, and we would share a surprise face, like we had no idea what was gonna happen, and then giggle after she was gone. So though I never feared Dad would ever hurt me when he was drinking, I did fear what went on between him and Mom when he was drinking.

They were a toxic, deadly mix to one another—especially on this particular and final day. Gandy, Mom, Sarra, and I raced to the big ole train station and the beautiful window that I learned would frame our future. Little did I know, it would be our last trip to the bustling railroad yard. Only the memory of the ornate window and its massive wood would remain a part of my life.

Mom stood in her worn, faded cotton dress and desperate expression, pathetically begging for Dad's check. The kind clerk, with empathetic blue eyes, read my mother's pleas then, as softly as possible, attempted to cushion the devastation once again, as in times past.

Without condescension, as if to soothe my mother's soul, the clerk rhythmically said, "I'm sorry, ma'am, Mr. Kelly picked up his pay first thing this morning."

The clerk might as well have been saying, "Mr. Kelly is as good as dead," because that's what I realized as Mom left that railway station with every ounce of her body filled with a threatening rage, which exuded from every cell of her being.

She was past anger, past rage; I am sure she was seeing red. We never ascended Franklin Avenue Hill so rapidly. No words were spoken. No explanations given. Mom took boards from the cellar and barred the entryways to the house—the cellar door, the side door, the front porch door. Only the hammering of nails into the wood preventing entry into the house could be heard above her breath of anger. When she had completed the task of barring us inside and barring Dad out, it was well past dark.

She sat waiting; we sat waiting. And we waited and waited for whatever the night ahead held. I wasn't sure what it all meant, but somehow the thickness of the atmosphere and the apparent rage and disgust that my mother was feeling set the tone for us all—to be quiet and to not question anything she was doing, nailing us inside that house, a house that felt more like a danger zone than a home. As the night became later and later, Becca took me to bed with her. I curled up by my big sister, falling asleep.

Late into the evening, the night's silence was pierced through with relentless banging on our doors, doors that would be barred from allowing Dad to enter. Screaming and yelling started, filling the night with the pent-up rage of the day and the life Dorothy was sick of living. Cursing exploded as the two parents volleyed back and forth—one in a drunken state, the other in a state of uncontrolled fury.

"Dorothy, open the door!"

"Go to hell. And get out of here, I never want to see your face again! Get out of here, Frank."

"I'm not going anywhere, open this damn door."

"I told you get out, and I mean it. I'll shoot you, Frank, if you come in here."

"Don't you threaten me, just open this door."

"I swear to God, Frank, you aren't coming in here. Go stay with that floozy Leapin' Lena you spend all your money drinking with. Don't come running home to me drunk and broke anymore."

A pause of silence, then glass shattered, screaming escalated. The broken glass all over the floor, Frank entered through a window. I heard Dad and Mom. I knew it was dangerous for them. Obviously, Becca knew the danger too. She hid me under her bed and crawled under the bed, curling up next to me, hiding us both. The fighting continued. Mom was furious. I couldn't tell if they were sobs of hysteria or resignation to murder. She had a gun when we were waiting. What was she thinking now?

"I'll kill you, Frank, if you don't get out of here."

Maybe Frank didn't believe Dorothy would do such a thing, but I had no doubt of it. I had seen her throw forks that stuck out of his skin before. I saw broken dishes flying at him. This time she was armed with Benn's hunting gun. What would she do? Dorothy's bloody cries pierced the night like a blade slicing through dark layers of fear; layers and layers of massive fear penetrated all of us. Benn went out his upstairs closet window to the part of the porch roof closest to the front lawn, where he could jump to the grass yard below. By the time he reached the street, neighbors had already helped him and intervened by calling for the police. And a shot was fired. Later, I learned the shot was more a serious "don't come near me or I'll shoot you" warning. She hadn't shot Dad, but he was taken away by the police, and she was questioned as well. Whatever happened with them, I don't know—except Dad never lived with us ever again in our green house on Franklin Avenue, and Mom never talked about that night or him again. Our trips to the railroad pay window were history, and so was my life with my dad.

He was gone, just like that. He never entered that home again. I heard later he moved to another state.

When Gandy and I were older and Dad would try to visit us, Merlin made it next to impossible with his cruel ways for anyone to be at ease visiting. Even as a youth, I could see the tactics Merlin used to humiliate and keep my father at bay. There would be no bonds formed or expression of love shown.

Merlin would rule, and that's all there was to it. He moved in to 503 Franklin Avenue, the green house Grandfather Kelly helped my mother buy. Merlin came too soon after Dad was gone. And Dad was gone.

CHAPTER 7

AT FIRST, IT WAS ALL peaches and cream. That's how it is with every groomer—toy trains and toy china tea sets, stuffed animals, typewriters, bicycles, shoes, even new school clothes. Then after the guard is down and the trust has been established, it's time to take possession. That's exactly what he did. He owned my mother and her children. We no longer stood in the welfare lines, needing or getting surplus.

We had a real washing machine. We had furniture that matched in our living room and books and food and a car. It even had a name: the Green Hornet.

We would take rides on Sunday afternoons—proud to be like everybody else, out taking rides and stopping to get ice cream. Paydays were spent going to the grocery store, not paydays that left us standing at a pay window, begging and hoping to God the check hadn't been drunk up. And it all looked so nice from the outside looking in. He changed our social class. But the cost of money costs too much sometimes. No one knew the price we were really paying. But one at a time, my siblings paid and then one at a time left the madness of the life we now had to live with Merlin as our new father. Since I was the youngest, I watched and I listened. I watched them be abused, and then they were gone. One by one, they were abused and then they were gone.

It started with my brother Benn, the oldest of Dorothy's sons. He didn't get the sweet treatment the other kids got initiated with. He was narrowed out, became the targeted child. He didn't get the niceties, not even verbally. He was constantly reminded that he was "no damn good." He was just like his father, who never amounted to anything. Benn had to buy his own way, earn his own keep, and was belittled every chance Merlin had to degrade him. It hurt my heart to hear the damning words and the ridicule Merlin poured out on my big brother. It was confusing to me. How could someone so nice as Merlin be so mean to Benn? Why, Benn was fun and loving and kind and wouldn't hurt a soul. Didn't Merlin know how good Benn truly was? This was a dilemma for my young mind. But I would soon learn the reality of the facade Merlin hid behind after months of his condescending nature to my brother.

The table was set. Evening was setting in too. Outside, the rustling leaves were whipping briskly with the wind's fingers picking them up and dropping them like wishes to the ground. Shadows started falling where once sun shone. It was getting darker. The day's events were over, and it was dinnertime. Becca had set the table, including a place for Benn. Merlin walked into the kitchen, cigarette in his hand.

"Where's that damn ashtray?"

"Oh, I moved it to set the table," Becca sang out.

"Put it back, now!" he demanded.

Obediently, Becca scurried to the counter to retrieve the ashtray and set it next to Merlin's plate. The aroma of Italian spaghetti sauce and Dorothy's homemade bread filled the air. With the finishing touches for dinner completed, Dorothy sat down by Merlin as she called, "Suuuuppperr's ready."

One by one, the table filled with hungry faces, excited to talk of the day and have heaps of spaghetti and meatballs in between each chatter. Benn usually worked evenings, and so it was nice to have him home for dinner with us. But something didn't feel right to Mary Pat. Something felt wrong.

Was it that Merlin was just unhappy about his ashtray? *That couldn't be it*, she told herself. Why was the atmosphere so tense? After all, it was a beautiful fall evening and the supper smelled so yummy and the kids were happily talking. *What am I feeling?* Mary Pat instinctively felt everything.

She had learned to read an atmosphere as if it was a newspaper ever since Merlin came to live with them. She had to be aware, alert, cautious. Something was stirring. The sounds of supper and the children's dialogue continued.

"Sarra, did you see my white sneakers? I need the shoe polish you used last night," Becca said.

"Shoe polish isn't gonna help those dirty white sneakers of yours!" Sarra chided.

"Yes, it will. I use it all the time."

Then someone told the story about the guy downtown who got arrested for stealing bank deposits by setting up a contraption that caught the deposits in a fishing net when they were deposited in the slot at the bank. You could hear the laughter over the silliness of the idea, catching money in a net! Gandy got the biggest kick out of it!

More interacting between the siblings, then Benn said, "Pass the spaghetti please."

Instantly, the laughter and conversations ceased and evil manifest. Out of nowhere, Merlin turned into a raving maniac, fierce with rage; and then seriously, all hell broke loose! Merlin stood up at the end of the table where he had been seated. He glared directly at Benn at the other end of the table and snapped, yelling full force, "Oh, pass the spaghetti, huh? Pass the spaghetti! I'll pass the spaghetti, all right. This is my house and my spaghetti. You get your lazy ass away from my table and my food," piercing Benn with his obvious hate and distain for him.

Right then, Benn had enough of Merlin's exhaustive condemnation. Defiantly, he lashed back, "I earn my own keep. I helped pay for this spaghetti, and it's mine too, and I'll eat all I want."

Instantly, without so much as a blink, Merlin picked the table up off two legs, angling the table and shoving it so violently that all the food, glasses, plates came crashing to the floor and shattering. Within seconds, a physical altercation was happening. The fight went from the kitchen, thrashing into the living room. Merlin had no chance against Benn's youth and strength. But it was Benn who showed himself to be the real man 'cause he was the one who stopped in the midst of all the chaos, screaming and yelling, and just left, walked away—more like he "ran away"—out the door and into the October night. He never lived with us again. He was gone. My big brother was gone. Mom went into her "let's act like nothing happened" mode. Benn was never mentioned, and he never did come home to us for years and years and years. He was a grown man in an Air Force uniform the next time I saw him. Dorothy continued to appease Merlin, and figuratively, when he said, "Jump," she said, "How high?" I didn't know about that. I couldn't figure that out, but I did know no man would ever separate me from my son if I ever had one.

Fall turned into winter, and Jack Frost frequented our nights. Not much changed. I learned to be seen and not heard. I studied everyone and everything around me. Though I was growing older, I never lost the curiosity of my youth. By this time, it was pretty clear that Merlin wanted Dorothy as a wife but he didn't want her children; we were all a burden for him. He used us as slaves, including Dorothy. She waited on him hand and foot. He couldn't even clean up his own cigarette ashes, which he haphazardly flicked into his big ashtray at the end of the couch that he occupied religiously. Ashes were always on the floor wherever he sat, and he took for granted that someone, and not him, would be cleaning them up. It appeared Merlin had stopped pretending now that he even liked the children at all.

It seemed he did things that were unjust simply for the sake of being mean or unkind. He started projects around the house at 503 Franklin Avenue, and it was the children and Dorothy who did the manual labor. He told Dorothy how to, and then she and the children did the work. Plaster was taken down one room at a time, the lathe exposed, and sheet rock replaced the old walls. All the rooms in the house were remodeled one room at a time by Dorothy and her kids. There was always work to do. There was not to be playtime for Mary Pat at her friends', Mickey and Christine's, anymore. Gandy was not allowed to go to the creek and catch crawdads or be out in the woods playing behind our house. We had work and school, and that's how we were defined.

But Sarra hurt the worst during this period of our lives. She worked hard and had calluses most of the time on her hands. But her deepest scars came when Merlin decided to tell Sarra that he was her real father. She was thirteen years old when she found out. She became angry. She didn't like that Dorothy had lied to her for thirteen years and that this man who was purely cruel was now letting her know. He was her father. So it was that our stepfather, Merlin, was actually her real father from an affair he and Dorothy had years prior. Now Sarra was finding out that she had half sisters and a half brother from Merlin's previous marriage. Her saving grace in it was that she bonded well with one of Merlin's daughters, Emma, and at a tender age of fifteen, met her and found great solace in their friendship. Their lives became closely knit and remained that way. But Sarra never bonded with Merlin. She hated him, and she hated Dorothy. She believed they were evil and brought the worst out in each other. That was a fact.

It was a warm spring day. The tips of yellow crocuses peeked their heads through the dampness of winter past. The air was filled with sounds of renewal as birds chirped, welcoming warmer air. The red robins bopped along—head up, head down—through the four grass tiers that layered our back lawn. Each tier represented a flat grassy level on the sloping hill, which eventually led down to the woods and then to the creek below. Our dog, Tippy, chose this day to run away from his dog coop in the backyard. I can't say that I blamed him; it was a perfect day for running away and breaking all chains—except, he broke loose with his chain still fastened to him. He returned but came home without his chain—or at least, that was the excuse we were given for the outrageous behavior that was soon to follow by Merlin and my mother, which eradicated any peace or beauty of that perfectly beautiful spring day. So we were told that Tippy lost his dog chain, and it was our duty to "find it."

Lining up one by one, Becca, Sarra, Gandy, and Mary Pat stood stiff and at attention before Merlin. In his regimented tone and manner, orders were spewed out—which basically came down to "Find the dog chain, or else!" We all scattered, frantically searching every inch of the yard in hopes of the find. Since I was the youngest,

MARY PAT KELLY UPRIGHT

Becca told me to stay in the backyard and not to go down into the woods near the creek. I'm sure she had flashback thoughts of our little brother drowning at the river and was protecting me from any mishap at the creek, which tended to flow quite aggressively at the spring melt-off of snow. The other children scattered, leaving the back lawn and heading down into the woods and closer to the swift water's edge, each taking a section going into the wooded area. There I stood in the backyard among the grassy tiers, combing the blades of grass for the lost dog chain. Some time passed, and when I looked up at the back of the green shingled house, staring out their bedroom window were the heads of Mom and my stepfather, Merlin.

Only their heads showed as they peered through the curtains, looking at me, glaring, which seemed very odd to me. I thought to myself, *What were they up to, what did they want, what had we done?* Fear gripped my young heart. I knew something not good was coming; however, at the time I had no idea how "not good" it was going to end up being. All of a sudden, Merlin was on the back porch, barking for all of us, "Get up here, now!"

My siblings must have heard his ranting as they came running like troops up the hill to the house, where Merlin was waiting with his razor strap—the leather-worn one we were often punished with, beaten for whatever he decided we needed a beaten for. I was the youngest, so I was first to get it. He marched me upstairs to my bedroom that was in the back corner of our house. I truly was paralyzed by fear and the anticipation of knowing a beating was coming. I had been through these kinds of terrors plenty of times. This one trumped them all. He had this sick-looking stare in his eyes. I was too young to define it as lust. I only knew that glazed-over, distant look in his eyes petrified me and made me feel scared. He started his orders in his sick voice, "Take off your clothes." I started to just take my pants off 'cause I knew he was going to hit me with the strap on my bare bottom. It wasn't okay. He didn't just want my pants down. He ferociously said, "All of them, take off all of them!"

I had to strip completely nude in front of him as he stared like a wild, glazed-over animal at me, stripping down to my third grade nudity. My breasts were starting to form, and I remember feeling embarrassed because I was starting to get some hair in private places and it was shameful for me having him see me this way. I was so embarrassed and so afraid. He made me face him as he stood there, staring at me in the nude. I was filled with a flood of emotion—disgust, shame, fear, worthlessness, my innocence attacked. I didn't know where to put my eyes. Where was I supposed to look? Why was he staring at my private parts, looking at me this way? What did all this mean? What was going to happen? Out of fear, I whimpered like a baby, but not too loud 'cause I was afraid what crying out loud might cost me. But my fear wouldn't let me be silent. I ached to whimper audibly.

"Shut up, lie on the bed."

I lay facedown across the edge of the bed, and he began swinging that strap high over my body, beating and beating and beating me. My mind weakened. There was no order to my thoughts. They bombarded me like bullets, triggering one panicked thought after another. My flesh ached. My heart shattered in a million irretrievable pieces.

He breathlessly blurted out, "Stand up." I stood, trembling with an overload of pain, fear, and panic. He showed no mercy.

"You know why you're getting this, don't you?"

"No, sir."

"All right then, you'll get some more until you can tell me why you're being punished."

Back on the bed, more lashes with the razor strap—more pain, fear, and embarrassment. But now I was doomed for sure because I absolutely had no inkling of an idea of why I was being punished. And with no answer, this felt hopeless to me. He beat me, and he beat me, and he beat me some more—asking in between the lashes if I had "figured it out yet."

Again, answering as before, "No, sir," I started fading. Finally, he commanded me to stand up and put my clothes on. While I was weakly and sorely dressing myself, he informed me that I needed to learn to obey, and that is why I was being punished. Then he proceeded to say that he had told me to look for the dog chain and I stayed in the yard instead of going into the woods with the others to find the chain. I had "disobeyed."

I tried to explain, "Becca told me to stay in the grassy area so I would be safe from the woods and creek."

He laughed a disgusting laugh and mocked me, "You don't do what she tells you to do. You do what I tell you to do. Now get out of here."

With that, I left my bedroom—emotionally, mentally, and physically crushed—headed back down the stairs, never to be the same. But little did I know, the horror had just begun. The groomer had come to reap his catch. One at a time, he called my siblings up the stairs. I don't know what disgust they faced or what excuse he gave them for wanting them to strip in front of him and get beaten, but whatever it was, I knew by the look in his face, it had nothing to do with disobedience; it had to do with that crazed animal look in his eye.

By the time the beatings got to Becca, my oldest sister's turn to be beat, I sat mummified at the bottom of the stairs that led to the room of the horror upstairs. I was too young to fully understand exactly what was happening. I only know I heard my sisters' and my brother's cries, and honest to God, I have never ever been the same since. I heard her plead and beg and scream for him to stop. I don't know what he did to her. I only know with the look he had in his eye, I couldn't begin to imagine what fear he must have caused my sister or what pain she faced. I did know, though, he was beating her, and I had no way of escaping what I heard; I was too young. I counted and counted and counted the strap hitting her until I could take no more and fled into our kitchen, where my mother was acting like nothing was going on. I started begging and pleading with her, "Please go get Becca, go help her, he's hurting her, and he's doing something to her, help her, help her please, make him stop, Mom, please." I pulled on her apron.

Her response was as scary as his actions, "Mind your own business, and go sit down."

I returned to the bottom of the stairs where I could still hear her, but I felt helpless, not being able to do anything for her, not being able to help her or rescue her or make him quit—my sister's cries etched in my soul.

"Oh my god, oh my god, please, please, help."

As her little sister, I felt my loyalty to her, and the best I could do was sit as close to her as I could at the bottom of those stairs. Somehow, it felt like I had to I couldn't abandon her. After her beatings and his atrocities concerning her, she returned to the living room; her back was bloody and hurting. She was in severe pain, and all Merlin did was give his dictated command—no remorse, no sign of his pent-up anger. He, as spent as I had ever remembered him, just ordered my mother, "Get her some salve for her back, Kid." That was his pet name for our mother, Kid. She responded to it well. Becca got some salve. But the DA found that not to be enough!

I'm not sure how it all came into the light—although I believe someone heard me pleading into the air on those stairs for my sister and her cries. However it happened, the school nurse saw the evidence of the beatings. There were legalities and a court session that followed. I didn't attend. I was too young, and so was Gandy, to go on the stand. But my sister Sarra wasn't, and they placed her on the stand in front of the monster that she would have to go home with after the hearing. She heard our mother's testimony.

Mom lied for Merlin, stating that she "wasn't there and didn't know how that happened to Becca."

Sarra was terrified, knowing she had to go home with them after the trial. She lied too, always feeling guilt for the fear she felt that caused her to minimize the beatings we all took that day. Becca was taken from us. Just like that, she was gone. My heart never recovered from the pain I felt, hearing and seeing my sister being abused. She didn't come back home. I missed her greatly. She really loved me as a little sister, and I loved her. I felt a void within me with her out of our home. She had been my "soft place to fall." She was ten years older than me, and she loved me like a little sister needs to be loved. But I was glad her abuse was over and that she was someplace safe— far from the fear of our home and the lives we lived, with a man and woman who really cared less and less each day for the children they lived with.

Dorothy didn't seem to stick up for her own kids, yet she would be the first woman to help a stranger in need—the first one to donate baked goods for a cause or help the poor. It was a paradox—more like a nightmare at times. There were still three children left in the house. Little did I know, it could get worse.

And really, what was my mother thinking anyway? What had happened to her? Where was her heart and her care for her children? Was food on the table and a payday worth all this to my mother? Wasn't life more than food and a change in social status? Where had she gone, the mother I knew once? Merlin possessed her now. She wasn't ours anymore. She showed her true colors and her loyalty when she lied on that stand before the court. It wouldn't be the last thing she closed her eyes to for his and money's sake. But I felt like I still loved her. She was my mother. She was the lady I stood in the surplus line with, the lady I missed Richie with, the lady who made it possible for me to be birthed and have life. I still loved her, though I understood her less and less. Was this what domestic violence did to a person? Was she as afraid of him as we were but didn't know it was fear that entangled her to her loyalty to him? Did she even know how to do anything else? Wouldn't human nature tell you what was normal and what was abuse? Did she even care? We couldn't trust her anymore, though, or depend on her for our protection.

She couldn't even protect herself. Somewhere within my heart, it felt as if she needed us to protect her too. But she would have nothing to do with that. She wasn't interested in any team but Merlin's. From an outsider looking in, Merlin looked good. He had a good job and position on the railroad. He definitely changed the social class Dorothy and her kids were used to. He was intelligent, an avid reader, a good conversationalist with others, loved history and politics, liked vacationing in interesting places on the East Coast, enjoyed camping, hated religion, drove a nice truck, and sported a crew cut! Sounds harmless, right? You should never judge a book by its cover. Man looks on outward appearance, but God looks on the heart. I became really good at reading the hidden.

CHAPTER 8

NOT LONG AFTER BECCA WAS taken and gone from us because of the abuse, we moved from our green shingled house at 503 Franklin Avenue in Susquehanna to a small rural town in the country, Starrucca, Pennsylvania. I loved living in Starrucca. In the 1960s, it was a sweet village. It looked like something from a Currier and Ives painting or the setting for the movie *Simon Birch*. It was wonderful! Our house was next to the ball field. We had two stores in the center of town. One store was about as old-fashioned as you could get, with all the wooden shelves behind a thick hardwood counter where the cash register was a notepad for the adding and subtracting, and the storekeeper used a long wooden pole that extended to clasp boxes or goods that were kept on the highest shelves. And there were these beautiful little wooden drawers with brass knobs that held buttons, rolls of lace, threads, ribbon—whatever was needed. The other side of the store displayed such stock as fancy scarves for ladies or writing paper or the latest farm gloves for the working man. All of it was just so perfect to me. I felt like I entered a story every time I walked through the doors. The jingle bells on the doorknob warned of your entrance, and usually, there was only one person at a time in there. The owners were always glad to see you and always glad to chat! When you didn't need to stop in the store but just had to walk by on your way to the post office, there would be the big fluffy cat, Charger, basking in the sun of the wide front window, caring not at all if you ever came into the store or not. He wasn't going to move for you or anyone else! He had sunning to do! I don't ever remember him doing anything but lounging in that window—a fixed live figure in the center of town!

The other store was a grocery store with old wooden floors and wooden shelves, a big glass-covered meat case that carried cold cuts and fresh meat and jars of pickles and peppers and big blocks of cheese from the butchers shop, and there were breads, condiments, canned goods, and such. Things were simple, one of everything you needed, and you didn't need ten choices for one product. Old Barney, a Bassett Hound, sat outside on the steps; and he—like Charger, the cat—didn't care one bit about your coming or going! He had sleeping to do!

We had one gas station, which looked like a laid-back version of the Seven Dwarfs' place. It was small, but everybody enjoyed being there. It had a little wood stove that kept us warm on snowy mornings waiting for the school bus. The oak wooden penny candy case was a main attraction. All the candy was a penny apiece—unless you bought red candy nickels and they were two for a penny! If you were lucky enough to have earned fifty cents shoveling walks, you could buy candy bars or chips or soda from the Coca-Cola bin, which was a metal tub that had ice in it and held cold drinks. There was a coffeepot for the men who stood around the wood stove and gabbed. And when you pulled in to get gas, somebody pumped your gas and washed your car windows. And if you couldn't pay this week, there was a tab and you could pay next week.

There were three churches in town, and all their lots were always filled with cars parked around them on Sunday Mornings. During the weekends, one of them usually had a chicken biscuit dinner going on or a pancake breakfast or a strawberry ice cream social— something of that nature. In the winter, it was okay to Christmas carol, and no one complained about the name of Jesus or a manger set out—in fact, local farmers donated hay for the manger and hayrides for caroling. Then everybody would stop and be treated to hot chocolate at one of the churches. There was a local Starrucca Hall, which looked like a big barn. A band would play on Friday nights, and most of the townspeople would come out for the music even if they didn't dance. There would be good food and clean fun! I learned to square-dance and polka in that hall and came to realize what a great tranquilizer music and dancing could be for a hurting youth's soul. The locals used it for wedding receptions and birthday celebrations, even the annual Halloween parade for the little ones. Teams got together to play basketball in the hall. It was a meeting place for just about anything you wanted to use it for. Families and kids gathered in it frequently. There was a funeral parlor right in the middle of town and an Agway on the hill into the village where the farmers could get supplies. But one of my favorite places in the little village was the swimming hole at the old arched stone bridge. It was where the youth gathered on hot summer days and where dreams were born and shared on the banks near the fresh running water. Gandy and I were allowed a half-hour swim for our break from our chores during the summer. It was a great escape. I cherished those times.

The village of Starrucca was a godsend in my life. The farms and green pastures, the hay and cornfields, the streams in the woods, the springs from the mountains, the hills with maple, oak, evergreens, birch, all kinds of beautiful trees, made the landscape a great refuge. I loved the sound of the church bells ringing in the valley mornings and the clatter of the wheels of the train every night as it rounded the big curve and crossed through our mountains, comforting me at the end of every day. The trains' whistle and rhythm was like clockwork. I could be lulled asleep by it. I loved the wildlife that surrounded the village too and lived in the mountains around us. It was different than the town we had moved from, and I cherished the nature of the village setting. I could leave the insanity of the house I lived in and find solace all around me. The mountains and the woods and the creek and the stars—all felt like home.

I knew the village well, and the families that lived there too, because I was the "paper girl." I had a paper route, delivering the newspaper on weekends and every morning before school. In the summer, I helped on a local farm, loading the bales of hay from the fields on to the hay wagon. Then we would ride the loaded wagon back to the barn and unload the wagon, while drinking ice-cold lemonade, with the ice and lemons floating in the glass jug. The condensation from the glass was cooling and soothing to our hot, callous hands. Haying wasn't like work at all to me because I got paid for it! The work I did at home for Merlin was much harder than the farmwork I did or the paper route I had. Merlin was very good at reminding me my pay for the work at home was a roof over my head and food on the table.

He scared me to death, even if he did feed me and give me a roof to live under. I never once felt the price we all paid to live with him was worth it. I lived on edge every minute with him. I was a nervous kid. I became grateful for the village and the nature around it. I didn't know until later that God was in the mountains, in those hills, from "whence cometh my help." I didn't know what to call it. I just knew it was a peaceful feeling, and it calmed my nerves. It was all too much living with Merlin and Mom. But outdoors—under the stars or swimming in the creek or running in the fields or singing in the Catholic church or singing in the Baptist church—all of it became my tranquilizer whenever I could escape being "under his roof." In those places, I would come to know a Holy Ghost that had no intention of ever leaving me or giving up on me, even when I gave up on myself. I had no name back then for who or what I felt. I only knew that going to school, going to work, going to church, going anywhere was always a refuge. It got me out of our house, gave me something good in life and comforted my soul.

Dorothy wasn't a woman who primped. She was quite the opposite. She presented tough both inside and out. She wore her clothes until they were frayed and stained; typically, they were both. Once, she fractured her ankle working outdoors. She slipped, twisting it in an irrigation ditch. She wrapped it in an ACE bandage and went through the swelling and the limping until it healed, never complaining once audibly about the pain that was obvious on her face. She never wore eye makeup; in fact, she hated it.

She didn't paint her nails or spend money on herself for any luxuries, dainties, or extras. It was the basics for Dorothy. Her biggest extravagance would be lipstick if there was a special reason to wear it.

Except this once, she decided to go past the basics, going to a salon to get a permanent for her hair. It went over like a lead balloon with him. The one time she dared to step out and do something pleasant for herself, he had to rob her of any joy or sense of satisfaction she may have had in how truly nice she looked.

He sat at the breakfast table, smoke circling the room from his Raleigh cigarette, ashes hanging from the lighted end ready to fall wherever they wanted to. His newspaper was lying spread open in front of him, his dirty dishes from breakfast pushed aside, as steam from his coffee cup sent an aroma that outweighed the Raleigh. The smell of coffee could have been coming from the percolator that sat on the stove. It didn't matter what smell was in the atmosphere or where it was coming from because it was clear from the tension in the air and the look on his face that Merlin was angry. Mary Pat walked into the house from feeding the chickens; it was bright and early in the morning. Dorothy was crying. Neither of them, Merlin or Dorothy, seemed to care that Mary Pat entered the kitchen right in the middle of an obvious quarrel between them.

"It's a damn waste of money!" he snarled. I work hard for my money, and you don't care, you go out and spend it on some foolish-looking hairdo. It looks like hell. If you cared anything about me…" Merlin paused. "You don't give a damn about me. No, you're too damn selfish to think of anybody but yourself and that good-for-nothing head of yours!" Merlin kept blurting out the verbal vomit of words, cutting Dorothy and her new perm down.

The norm would be, Dorothy would say nothing in response and just take his projected vomiting of insults and disdain—not this time. My mother took a cup of hot coffee, heaving it and splashing it out across the counter where she was standing five feet from Merlin.

She grabbed a pair of shears from the basket nearby and ran into the bathroom, screaming, "You son of a bitch, you dirty son of a bitch, you'll get your money!" Mom returned with a paper bag full of beautiful waves of black hair and threw the bag at Merlin. "Here, take your goddamn money, you son of a bitch. Now, now you explain to people what the hell happened to my good-for-nothing head!"

Mom had cut all her hair off as close to the scalp as she could get it; not one curl remained. She cut it a chunk at a time, and it stuck out all over. Dorothy wasn't done.

"I hope you're satisfied, and you can bet your fat lazy ass, I won't ever be spending a penny of your precious hard-earned money to look decent! You're the one who's gotta look at my good-for-nothing head. Try explaining that to your precious railroad buddies."

Merlin never responded. Not a word.

Oh, no, I thought, *she is gonna pay big time for this one.*

His facade of passiveness was just that—a facade.

I saw her bruised before and covering up where the bruises came from, coming to the table with swollen eyelids and puffy face. This would not go without cost. He would not wink at her self-defense.

Mom stormed out of the kitchen. It was over, at least for now, at least until that night when I heard her crying in bed. I had heard her cry from their bedroom several times. He would be droning a way about us kids and how we all take advantage of him and whatever else he wanted to bitch to her about in his muffled baritone droning as he creeped me out in an otherwise still night. Her hair took a long time growing out; it was embarrassing. I felt sorry for her—not for how ridiculous her hair looked, but for the fact that she couldn't see how outrageous our lives and hers were and do something about it.

CHAPTER 9

I HAD A LOT OF nice friends in Starrucca. Nancy, my best friend, lived closest; only the ball field separated our homes. We were in the same grade at school and shared a lot of the same interests.

Nancy's mother, Margaret, was influential in exposing me to culture and interesting history surrounding the local towns and other villages. Margaret would take us girls to women's breakfasts or special speakers representing talks about clean water or protecting the wildlife. Nancy hated it and felt dragged to these "stupid places and stupid speeches." But Nancy loved her Mom, and when Margaret turned fifty, it was Nancy who convinced me that we should make a special surprise birthday cake for Margaret. There was a column every week in the local paper entitled, "Straight from Starrucca."

Margaret wrote the column. Every submission ended with, *Cheerio!* And every column told of the sweet happenings in a little village hidden away in the mountains outside of Susquehanna. No family was excluded—every birth, every visitor, every graduation, every change of season was written, and all the happenings around every season were told "Straight from Starrucca and Margaret's heart."

I thought of her as a great role model. Besides, I was sure Margaret loved this little village as much I did! Margaret was always the one that wrote about the little yellow-winged bird at the bird feeder, or the finely dressed chickadee, or the red cardinal visiting on a snow-covered morning. Margaret recognized and encouraged my academic interest and success. It was Margaret, and not Dorothy, that gave me positive feedback and spoke kindly into my life of my talents and abilities. I was never sure if it was because Margaret herself was a teacher or if it was a personal interest in me to succeed, but it didn't matter. Someone cared, and I was going to latch onto that care. It was Margaret who was always proud of my report card and academics.

It was November 22, 1963. All the Catholic students were taken from the public school and walked down to the local fire hall in Thompson for religious instructions. On the way back to the schoolhouse, after the completion of our catechism lesson, the attending teacher had us sit down on the stone wall in front of the school. He reported in a very shocked manner that President Kennedy had been assassinated! The sound of his words resounded loudly in my mind. It didn't make sense. I took for granted that everybody loved our president. I thought he was doing a great thing helping with equality of all people. I thought he cared—really, truly cared—about America. Why would someone want to shoot him? I cried and just stared out the window of the school bus on our twelve-mile ride home. I didn't know it then, of course, but the '60s were just getting ready to make a big splash in American history.

Martin Luther King Jr. and his freedom speech, "I've Got a Dream," his assassination, as well as Bobby Kennedy's, the Vietnam War, Woodstock, the Beatles, Bob Dylan, The Beach Boys, The Rolling Stones, the drug revolution—all rippled in history through the 1960s. Women's roles were changing with the introduction of the birth control pill. The "Leave it to Beaver" years were over, and I was there, growing into a teenager in the middle of it all.

I was deeply affected by President Kennedy's assassination. I was only ten years old then. I wrote a poem and sent it to Mrs. Kennedy. I received a correspondence in return—a letter edged in black, stating that my poem would be placed in a book and housed in the John F. Kennedy Library one day. It felt personal to me. I turned the poem into a song. My music teacher heard it and invited me to sing it at our choral concert that year, the spring of 1964. I was delighted, overwhelmed, but excited that I had been chosen for such a privilege. I was getting ready for the concert that night. We all wore black and white—girls, black skirts and white blouses; boys, black pants and white shirts. I had no accompaniment for the song I wrote; I would sing it a cappella. I finished my supper and my chores, dressed in my black-and-white, and was ready to leave for the concert. Mom was going to take me.

"Where you going all dressed up like a penguin?" his gruff, unkind voice bellowed at me.

"I'm singing in the choral concert at school."

"How are you getting there?"

"Mom is going to drive me. She's going to the concert too, to hear me sing the song I wrote about President Kennedy."

"No, she is *not*! You're going there just to show off. You're nothing but a show-off! She's not taking you anywhere! Find your own ride."

Mom stood silent, hands cupped. She looked me in the eyes. I turned and walked out, closing the door carefully behind me—in case he changed his mind and wouldn't let me go at all. I had to find someone who would drive me the twelve miles into the school. I really felt like crying.

But it was no time to be feeling sorry for myself. There must be other families going. I would hurry and find a ride to my school. I ran up to the center of our village and thought about who might be going to see their child tonight. I knew Penny was going. I would ask her mother if I could go with them.

Madeline, Penny's mother, was more than glad to take me. I caught them at the last minute, getting ready to leave. I thanked God. She was aghast that Merlin waited until the last minute and wouldn't let my mother drive me or go to see her "little girl sing."

"Why, she *should* be so proud of you!"

She was more struck with horror that Dorothy didn't go anyway, regardless of Merlin! But Madeline, or the others, didn't know the half of the horror that really went on in our home. I had to let it go. I couldn't make my mother's bondage or weakness my battle. I couldn't handle the emotional overload of it if I did. I was already feeling such rejection from Mom. It already hurt too much that neither I nor all my siblings had a safe place to just be. I couldn't think about it all then. I had to get ready to sing in a high school auditorium a song that I wrote and never sang in front of an audience before. With all the abuse I had seen already around me and to me, this situation of finding a ride and being rejected by Mom was just part of the norm for my heart. I knew I was really alone in the world—except maybe for that sense of comfort that washed over me at times, almost like a reminder that maybe I wasn't alone. Maybe someone or something really was watching out for me.

The auditorium was packed. The chorus sat tiered on a platform stage in the front of hundreds of people—sisters, brothers, mothers, fathers, friends, relatives, teachers. Excitement was in the air! Our music teacher stood before us, arms in directing motion to accent and direct every low and every high, every crescendo and every halt!

The chorus sang out, "I love to go a-wandering along the mountain path, and as I go, I love to sing, a knapsack on my back."

I was in pure joy! But I was also a bit afraid because I knew with each song we finished, I was drawing closer to the time that I would stand alone in front of all these people and sing my song! Doug, the boy that sat next to me in chorus, must have sensed some of my nerves, and he gently reminded me, whispering quietly, "Don't worry, you're gonna do a great job."

The next thing I remember, the room went silent. Ms. Corey then announced, "Mary Pat Kelly, singing a song she wrote in honor of our late President John F. Kennedy."

I walked to the center of the stage. I stood calmly, surprising even myself how right it felt being there. I looked out over the faces and the crowd before me. You could hear a pin drop as I began to sing, "On November the twenty-second the year sixty-three ..."

I finished my song, and before I even turned to go back to my seat next to my friend, people were standing, cheering. The whole audience rose to their feet in a wave of exhilarated clapping and gave a standing ovation to a little girl whose heart soaked in the acceptance. Bowing in gratitude, I was so thankful tears welled up in my eyes and in the eyes of my friends behind me. I thought to myself as I was returning to my seat, *If Mom could see me now.*

It was about this same age and time of my life that Merlin began to show behaviors that defined him as a sexual pervert to me.

I couldn't trust him for one minute, and I knew it. If I climbed a tree to look in a bird's nest, he would "pretend" like he was graciously helping me down and "just happened" to slip his hand up under my T-shirt and put his hands on my now-formed breasts—with me dismissing it and the embarrassment of it to me as nothing. Or he would chase us running in the yard and catch me and fondle me, pretending, "It's catch, it's how you play the game, you have to 'grab' the person to catch them!" So any complaint I made was in my own silence, my own dread. His tactics wouldn't be heard.

It was around this same time that my mother called Gandy and me together in what was called our middle room—'cause it was a room you entered when you came into the house and it was right in the middle of the kitchen and the living room. She sat us down in the same chair and then stood in front of us to tell us she had been to see a priest about finding a place for Gandy and me to live.

"WHAT!" I started crying, and Gandy told me to shut up.

Mom kept going with her announcement. Merlin and she had decided that it would be better for us to live somewhere else. So when the parish was back in touch with her, we would be going.

Oh, my heart, my heart. My heart sank. Silently, I considered, *Was this because I didn't want to go along with his little games?* I didn't know. But I did know for sure I was not ready to lose my mother. I had already lost Dad. I couldn't bear to lose her too. The parish never did take us, but I learned more than ever not to "stir the pot"—not to complain, not to mention anything, not to bring into the light any of his little sick games, or I'd be gone—just like that, I'd be gone. At age eleven, I was trying to understand the cost of having a mother. Giving her up was not easy.

The regiment of hard labor we did for Merlin continued. My sister Sarra took the brunt of that, being the oldest child left at home. They worked her like a workhorse. My brother Gandy too worked far beyond his age. So did I, but after seeing what my siblings went through, I only wanted to work harder to be as much a relief to them as I possibly could be, even though I was younger. Merlin had begun his "projects" of remodeling the house as soon as we moved into the house in Starrucca, and of course, it was all on Dorothy and the kids to do the work. He dictated what needed to be done and how to do it.

The old plaster came down with the old lathe; the Sheetrock went up. The plastering, the painting, the kids did it all. That was one of his little games too. I saw him use it twice against my siblings.

Prom night—a night in a young teen's life that should be a night of good memories, not agony and fear. But Merlin couldn't bear to see them happy. In the other reconstruction project, in the midst of all the plaster and dust, he made Sarra work up to half an hour before "finally" releasing her to get ready for her date. The thick dust that was in the air was ridiculous. Sarra had wrapped her hair in a towel, but it wasn't the same as being a teenage girl nice and fresh for your big night. He did everything he could to undermine any joy a child might have over the simple pleasures of being. So here we were again—different house, different teen, same game.

Gandy was told that he could use the family car for his prom date if he did his work. He worked until after dark in the plaster dust and grime of the remodeling. When it was the last minute, Merlin finally let him go to clean up. But when Gandy was ready for the car keys, Merlin—like the snake he was—recoiled for the attack and decided he couldn't use the car; he'd "have to find his own way."

Gandy panicked. He had asked a special girl in his class to be his date for the prom, and she had accepted! Now she would be ready and waiting for her escort to show up at her door and drive them off into their magical night! Gandy, dejected, ran into the dark night. I peered through the upstairs window, squinting through the condensation on the glass, searching in the darkness for my brother as he headed toward the village center to find a ride. How would he explain this to the teenaged girl waiting in the comfort of her living room for him? Why, why was Merlin so cruel? Did he take pleasure in his unjust, unfair, cruel tactics to us? What was his purpose for being so smug in his controlling manner?

My heart ached for my brother Gandy. I stood helpless, watching him disappear into the rainy, dark night, desperate. I knew the rain hid his tears. I found out later it was my eldest sister, Becca—the child taken from us for the beatings—who came to his rescue.

She, by this time, was married and lived about thirty miles from us, though we were not allowed to see her. Gandy called her. She and her husband, had just purchased a new Coronet. They readily allowed Gandy the use of it that night. He drove in like a prince to escort his princess to their high school prom, the end being the better! His date never did know the cost Gandy's heart paid that night and the blessing of that special ride to their prom! I felt, again, like someone heard the cries of my heart as I watched my brother fade into that rainy, dark night.

Could it be that something, someone, bigger than us was watching over us in spite of our circumstances?

CHAPTER 10

THOUGH SARRA AND I WERE never as close as Becca and I were, I still loved her with all my heart. I think the pain that I felt for all my siblings made me feel an unconditional love for them all. It was like watching their lives being controlled by a cruel circus master. All of us bound by his chains and his whips only made me feel more kindred to them. We shared a common bond of abuse. If no one else knew, we all knew; and we shared that knowing, even if we couldn't explain it to anyone else. You had to live in the dysfunction of the abuse to understand what life truly was like for us. We had each other. That's why watching them—my siblings, one by one—go through the final extreme act of abuse that would take them all from me was difficult. I heard my brother's cries. I heard my sister's cries. Sarra would be no different.

I was awakened by the gasps and sniffling breath of my sister. It was the middle of the night. I lay in a twin bed next to her, in the same bedroom. The hall door was cracked just enough to let the slim ray of light creep through into the darkness of the room. I was startled.

What was happening? What had happened? Why was she so distraught and crying, her cries waking me in the middle of the night?

"Sarra, what's wrong?" I asked.

"Shut up, before he comes back in here. Be quiet!" Sarra barked at me.

She continued her low whimpering in muffled cries from obvious brokenness and fear. About that time, *he* showed up at the crack of the door! I froze in my bed, completely still, as not to make a sign of life—his black silhouette outlined in the doorway.

Directing his indignation toward my sister, he blurted, "You better shut up that bawling, kid!" In an accusing tone, he rambled on, "What are you trying to do, wake up this whole house? If you do, there will be more where that came from. So your best bet is to shut up and go to sleep!"

He pulled the door shut all the way this time. Not even the sliver of light creeped through. It was utter darkness. I did not say a word. I hoped even my breathing couldn't be heard. My heart ached for her.

Sarra smothered her cries, stuffed her agony, and her gasps broke my heart as I lay helpless in the bed next to hers.

What had he done?

I didn't know, but I hated him. I hated him for making her cry and for making us all afraid in our own house. I heard every heart's cry, including my mother's, and felt like there was nothing I could do about it. It was like living in quicksand with no way out.

Reconstruction in the house moved into the dirt cellar. We would be putting a new cinder block wall under the house, giving it a new foundation, and expanding the cellar from a one-room dirt floor space to a full cinder-walled foundation under the entire house. It started with the digging and a makeshift ramp of plywood, used to roll the wheel barrels full of dirt out of the dark dirt space into a pile outside—one shovel at a time, one wheel barrel load at a time. The job took months. I was assigned the task of sorting through the excavated dirt to find the cobblestones and gray stones. Then I was to separate them and carry them with other rocks, creating a rock pile. I was sent to this rock pile often "to wash rocks." If I had no other chores left to do, my chore was to wash the rocks. He used them in the concrete and in other building projects around the outside of our house. The kids and Dorothy had put a new foundation under the house at 503 Franklin Avenue, and now they would do the same to this house. Only, with less kids to work now, the majority of the hard labor fell on Sarra, who was the oldest sibling left. She and Gandy carried the brunt of the work done in that dingy, dark, dirty one-room cellar—expanding it a pick and a shovel, wheel barrel full of dirt, day after day, load after load, at a time. I wasn't assigned the pick and shovel; I was assigned the job of tying a rope on the front of the wheel barrel and pulling forward on the load when the wheel barrel was full and needed to be pushed up the ramp out of the cellar. Sarra and Gandy took turns pushing the loaded wheel barrel up and out, and I pulled on the front with the rope.

The positive about it was, we were really strong, muscular kids! There wasn't a weak thing about us! We worked on that project regularly and steadily, day after day after day. It was always a relief when we would get a half hour to go to the stone bridge to swim. We welcomed the break from the hot sun and dirty work. Then one day, all hell broke loose during the digging of the cellar.

Sarra's abuse escalated to terror for me. Sarra was more verbal than Gandy and me. She could only hold in her silence so long, and then she would say what she wanted to, regardless of what it cost. Gandy and I were too afraid to say anything. I had learned it was better for me to be seen and not heard. It worked for me as a surviving technique. Dorothy used Sarra's need to speak up as an excuse to say, "Sarra deserved what she got." It appeared that Dorothy felt Sarra should take the abuse and be quiet about it—as if abuse was to be accepted without ripples or repercussions. Sarra had enough. She would have let them kill her just to finally have a voice to speak her truth about what she felt of their dysfunctional, sick behaviors. I was there watching.

It had been a hard day's work, as usual, but Sarra was physically exhausted and mentally drained. She had worked relentlessly in the cellar, and I could see the exhaustion on her; but knowing I couldn't do anything about it, I kept working. Sarra decided that she was going to take a break. Throwing down the shovel, she walked up the plywood plank from the dark cellar to the light of the outdoors in the afternoon.

Merlin was sitting nearby in his leisure position, cigarette dangling from his mouth, bobbing up and down as he bellowed in Sarra's direction, "Where do you think you're going?"

As nonchalantly as a Sunday stroll, Sarra looked at him in defiance and said, "I'm done!"

Needless to say, he had other things in mind, and what he perceived as her display of defiance to him went over with an explosion, "Like hell, you are! Get your ass back in that cellar."

"No!" She didn't budge. "You treat us like slaves! I'm done!"

I'm watching from the cave-like opening, peering from the cellar to the yard, where their interaction is happening. I have no idea what's going to happen next. I'm paralyzed with fear from the history of any resistance ever shown to his control. I'd watched what happened. This would not be different. But it was different; it was worse than anything I had ever witnessed—abuse so bad I still can see my sister's face and body as if it happened yesterday, his ranting in process.

"Oh, I treat you like slaves, do I? Well...I guess I'll have to show you how slaves are treated!" He was so smug. "Now, get your ass back here!"

She continued to walk away. He physically forced her back into the cellar and worked her harder than any time I've seen him force work on her before. But I knew it was only the beginning, and as a sibling watching this abuse, it was like waiting for the land mine to blow, knowing it had been stepped on. Dread, fear, anxiety, and stress permeated my soul. I was scared. I knew something awful was coming. He had only just begun to retaliate. I could hear him that night, lecturing my mother about Sarra's behavior and rebellion, as if it was her fault that Sarra didn't just take the abuse without happenstance. The old routine whine of his—about how Dorothy's kids never appreciate anything, how he took us from the welfare line, how we have a roof over our head and a decent meal and we don't appreciate anything, how Dorothy lets us get away with murder—it was a restless night.

The following day, he decided she would pay big time for her so-called defiance. He woke Sarra extraordinarily early and made her do all the housework alone, which typically, I shared in doing. He verbalized to her that he would "show her what a slave was treated like and see how she likes that."

Sarra went from the inside housework to the outside work of picking and shoveling, without help. No tying on the rope to help pull the loaded wheel barrel out of the dark, dank cellar. She pushed every load out alone. No brother Gandy to take turns picking then shoveling. He was instructed to wash rocks instead. She was on her own, carrying the brunt of all the hard labor. Her back was killing her. Sarra was showing signs of exhaustion, and Merlin could not have cared less. In fact, he gloried in her pain. She needed a break, and he was not about to give her one. He didn't let up on her one bit, for even a minute.

Gandy and I watched it all play out like a horror film. We kept doing our work at the rock pile, afraid to even turn our head the wrong way, look too long, pause too long, say anything. We were like robots.

With each push of the wheel barrel, Sarra was showing more and more exhaustion. She needed a break. He wouldn't give her one. It was obvious that Sarra would have to stop this frenzy of hard labor. The atmosphere swelled with fear. Merlin was just waiting trying to break Sarra's spirit to subjection to his every control. Then he would torture her some more. It was exactly what happened. Under the fatigue of the day's work and heat with Merlin playing the part of slave driver, Sarra exploded. She threw down the shovel for the last time.

With a determined glare, she looked him right in the face and made her emphatic statement, "I'm done! I'm not doin' any more of your work. Not now, not ever!"

He instantly struck back, "Pick up the shovel!"

"No!"

"I said, pick up the shovel!"

"And I said no. You'll have to kill me before I ever pick up your shovel again. I'm done!"

"You're gonna be sorry, kid!" he retorted.

"I don't care what you do to me. I'm never doing your dirty work again!" Sarra was adamant, sobbing.

Sarra walked past him. Even if it cost her life, she was done. I knew it; Gandy knew it. We feared for her life at that point. He was a monster, and the influence he had over Dorothy would soon show the manifest evil possible in our home. Merlin reacted with a hard backhand, hitting Sarra across her face. It knocked our sister to the ground. Sarra's face was bleeding. He picked her up by the hair of her head, struggling with her all the way into the house, never letting go of her scalp. Gandy and I could hear the explosion of voices and the thuds from inside the house. We kept working, petrified, acting as if nothing was happening, robots washing rocks, afraid to do anything but breathe.

I started crying. What's happening? What are they gonna do to her?

"Shut up. Stop it. You'll get us in trouble!" Gandy snapped.

"I'm afraid, Gandy!" tears poured down my face as I moved in the quicksand of our lives.

"Shut up right now, Mary Pat! I'll hit you with this rock, just shut up!" Gandy was overtaken with fear.

I did shut up. I kept it all inside. It was going to get worse.

Dorothy was inside too.

What could be happening? Oh, God, I'm so afraid for Sarra.

I wondered if God heard me. I kept washing rocks. Knowing Mom's position, I knew Sarra had no defense. There would be no one to defend her abuse. I cried. The voices escalated to hysteria.

Merlin was bellowing, "Now, get in there!"

More resistance, more banging, screams, thuds. We breathed the violence and terror of the air. I wanted to run. But where, where could I run? I cried harder. My tears caused Gandy more fear.

"Stop crying, just stop!"

I couldn't. I felt sick to my stomach, like I was going to throw up. I didn't know how to help my sister, how to stop this maniac, this insanity we were trapped in. What could I do? What was I supposed to do? I couldn't think clearly at all. I hated these rocks! I just felt like throwing them all through their windows and running and running and running and never looking back.

My thoughts streamed from my mouth, "I hate this place! I hate them! I hate living here! I hate being here!" I felt hysterical!

Gandy grabbed me by the shoulders and shook me violently, "Mary Pat, stop … stop it right now! Just do your work! Just do your work!"

He let go of my shoulders, and I could see the fear in him too. I could feel the resignation that we were two kids who couldn't do anything except be there right now. The violence continued pouring from every crack of the house. Sarra was inside, screaming. Mom was yelling. Merlin was hollering. Voices were shattering the air. The banging was so loud I couldn't help but wonder what was going on in there. I knew, though, that Sarra was getting beat with his razor strap. He was merciless with his beatings.

Suddenly, Sarra quit resisting externally; she held her excruciating pain inside. She had determined not to cry, not to give him any more satisfaction of knowing he hurt her. She went silent. The house went silent of her cries. She stilled, a repercussion of vibrating torture.

"How do you like that, kid?" he said as each lashing brought more pain. "That'll teach you who's boss and when to run your mouth and when to shut up!"

Sarra got sick to her stomach and started vomiting. She ran into the bathroom.

Dorothy was on her heels, telling her, "This is your own doing! You'll learn to do what you're told and keep your mouth shut! You're getting what you deserve."

We had all heard that one too many times. "We all deserved this." Standing in the bathroom door, Dorothy ordered her daughter Sarra back outside.

"I can't! I'm throwing up!"

"Get back outside right now if you know what's good for you!" Dorothy shoved Sarra out the door to where Gandy and I were.

Close to us was a giant boulder that had been excavated from the cellar project. Dorothy ordered Sarra to sit on that boulder and said, "Now, you sit there and bake!"

The sun was intense, the burning rays penetrated through each of us at that rock pile, as she ordered Sarra to the confines of that giant rock.

Sheepishly, I raised my head, taking in the surroundings of our lives. This was pathetic. Sarra was sweating profusely. She looked like she had been beaten to a pulp, eyes swollen, now lying out on that rock, vomiting over the edge, sick to her stomach. This was like a bad nightmare that I could not stop. It was our reality, and it was terrifying. Sarra's abuse affected me as badly as if it was my own abuse. Yet I could do nothing. And whatever could have been done, I wasn't aware of because I was still so young. I felt guilt over my siblings' abuse, all of them. Watching Sarra bake, it was like a video in my head of Benn's abuse and Becca's abuse and Sarra's abuse and Gandy's abuse—it flooded me with emotion.

Whatever we tried to do to stop the abuse just backfired into more retaliation, until the fear had total control, leaving us paralyzed and unable to think of a way out. I ran away once to escape the insanity; they found me and dragged me back home. I was made to stay in my room for three days, not even allowed to go to school, shut in like a wild animal would be. Now, here we were—caged, though we were all outdoors—watching this horrendous abuse go on. Mom's words to her very own flesh-and-blood daughter echoed in my mind, as she stood like a hawk on guard over her: "Now, you sit there and bake!"

Sarra was sick, and Dorothy didn't stop her from lying down. How could she? Sarra was puking her guts out, lying flat in that hot sun with her head over the edge of the huge boulder, lying there while ordered to bake in that intense heat of the day after a brutal beating. Sarra wasn't done—for now, maybe—but we had the rest of the day to live through. At the dinner table that night, the battle resumed full force.

Merlin—all cocky and proud of his victim, his power over her and everyone else under his reign—spoke, "Well, kid, how'd you like that? This is just how you wanted it, isn't it?"

Sarra, shocked at his words, didn't waste a second in response, "No! It's just how YOU wanted it! 'Cause you're sick and need a psychiatrist!"

Like a cobra striking, Mom defended Merlin, striking Sarra, smashing her right in the mouth and knocking her backward from her chair. Sarra hit her head on the edge of the tub behind her. She was stunned and bloody—all this at our dinner table, after a completely lunatic day. Sarra was drained. But it didn't stop her from wanting to retaliate against Mom.

Gandy started yelling, "Don't hit her, Sarra, don't hit her!"

I was afraid they—Merlin and Mom—were going to kill my sister.

"Now, get up!" Dorothy demanded in her voice that sent chills down my back.

Sarra defiantly, through bloody words, responded, "No, you put me here, you pick me up!"

By this time, Merlin had exited the house and gone up to the garden on the side hill just outside the kitchen door. Dorothy grabbed Sarra, lifting her up by the hair of her head and literally throwing her out the back door, causing Sarra to hit a steel post that was being used to brace the porch while construction was going on with the house's foundation. Seeing Sarra's face made me feel sick to my stomach. I thought I was going to pass out. I could tell that Sarra was terrified but determined she wasn't backing down.

Glaring at Dorothy, she lashed out, "Don't take your eyes off me because I swear I'm running away the first chance I get. You're as sick as HE is!"

Their verbal combat had come to a head.

"Get up there with Merlin right now, I've had enough of you!" Dorothy ordered.

Sarra walked up to upper garden under Dorothy's direction. Merlin was sitting in a lawn chair close to the garden's edge.

Seeing Sarra's face, he asked, "You had enough yet, kid?"

Sarra changed defense. Now she wasn't talking anymore—silence. She decided to be silent even when they addressed her and expected an answer. This defiance sparked more rage in them. He did not like it when he didn't have control. If he wanted you to talk, you were going to talk. But Sarra was not going to give into their power over her or give them control without a fight.

Seeing Sarra all bloody from Dorothy's beating to her, Merlin sarcastically added, "Hope you're happy now, kid, see what you've done to yourself?"

Sarra did not peep a sound, not a word. Instead, she stood up and started walking away, blood running from her nose and mouth.

"Where do you think you're going?" Dorothy glared.

Sarra replied, "To get a tissue."

Dorothy took a wadded one from her shorts pocket and threw it at Sarra. Sarra picked it up and threw it away defiantly.

"I'd rather bleed to death."

Silence followed.

Dorothy begged, "How do you like what you've done now?"

No answer—silence.

Merlin sparked up, "Is she giving you some more mouth?"

Dorothy said, "No, she has just decided she's not talking to me."

Merlin demanded, "You better answer her, kid, or how would you like some more?" as he handed the garden hoe to Dorothy, with a diabolical grin.

Sarra, still refusing to give them an inch of victory, said, "I'd love it, right here it is!" pointing to her chin and raising it in defiance to Dorothy.

That was it; that sent Dorothy into a frenzy—into a bloody frenzy! Dorothy tackled Sarra, sitting on her chest, hitting her again and again in Sarra's face. The rest of the night was a blur to me. I don't know how it ended or what happened after that.

I only know, the next morning, my brother Gandy told my sister, "You look like a caveman."

And she did. She was beaten so badly it was hard to distinguish her facial features. She was purple and blue and red and swollen. Her eyes were black and bruised, lips cut and distorted, and she was in pain, with no medical attention. Someone called the cops. Someone besides Gandy and I must have been watching the horror that went on outside the night before.

When the police arrived and saw Sarra's face all beaten black and blue, he asked in shock, "What happened to her, Dorothy?"

"She got mouthy with me, and I had to slap her."

"Now, Dorothy, you know that a lot more took place here than that." He started asking Sarra questions.

But under the watchful eye of Merlin, Sarra froze. The policeman noticed it. He took her into the police car and questioned her.

"Now, what happened here?"

Sarra, explaining the horror story, pleaded with the cops to take her away. The cop explained he couldn't—something about his jurisdiction—but he told Sarra he would send someone tomorrow who would take her. The policeman said someone from the county would come and help her leave there. He left; Sarra was left behind. No charges were brought against Merlin or Dorothy. But they didn't hit her or make her work; they left her alone.

The next day, Merlin asked her, "Do you want to leave?"

When she told him, definitely, she wanted to, he told her to pack her things and get out.

But against all common sense and justice, when the official county "lady" arrived, she didn't take Sarra from the house either. Sarra pleaded with her as well to be taken, but it seemed the "red tape" of a social service system that operated in the '60s weakened the hands of the county. It appeared that she couldn't take Sarra for two weeks—something about Merlin and Dorothy being her real mother and father. I was too young to understand it all and what the reality of it meant. Wasn't the abuse apparent? This only scared me more. Who would help us? There was a repercussion of that nightmare episode, though. The officials must have had their eyes on Merlin and Dorothy because they never beat Sarra again. They still were slave drivers, still unjust and cruel, perverted in their thinking, but they didn't beat her anymore. The cellar project got finished. The house had a full cinder block cellar under all the outside walls of our home—a project finished—and Sarra helped complete it. Within that year, Sarra turned eighteen, and as soon as she did, she ran away and got married. Her boyfriend picked her up at the school bus stop in the village on a February morning of her senior year.

My sister was gone and would never live with us again. Merlin put out an "all-points bulletin" through the police that night when Sarra didn't return home. She had run away and was successful at it. They couldn't stop her or bring her back; she was eighteen and free. An angel named Ken drove her out of that nightmare into a free world. Sarra was her own from then on. No one ever told her what to do, how to do it, or when to do it, ever again in her life. She was free.

CHAPTER 11

IT WASN'T LONG AFTER SARRA ran away that my brother Gandy went to live on a farm near our home in Starrucca. The couple was elderly and needed a hired hand. With the cellar project finished, Merlin insisted Gandy get a job. He was more than glad to. My brother rode his bike to their farmhouse, asked for the job, and was hired on the spot. He was offered the opportunity to stay there and have his own room because of the hours of milking. Gandy liked the farm, and the elderly couple truly loved having Gandy there to help them. It was a relief for Gandy; he later commented on how peaceful being on the farm and living away from home was. With Gandy out of the picture, Merlin took advantage of having me—the youngest and only child left—living with him and Mom. He needed a young girl to violate.

He started by pretending that my shoulders were out of place when I walked. He would make me lift my shirt and examine my shoulders, standing before him in my bra. His hands were monsters to me. I was afraid and poisoned by his touch. I had great anxiety and grew continually in fear. When I would try to get Dorothy (Mom) to help or intervene, she just made excuses for him.

"He's only trying to help you. He's no different than a doctor would be."

I thought, *Lies, lies, and more lies to condone him and dismiss me.*

It continued and became more and more invasive personally. Merlin would find reasons to punish me and send me to my room so he could get me alone. If I put the fork on the wrong side of the dish, if I talked too loud, if I had the wrong sweater on, if I had to be told to feed the chickens rather than just do it—all were excuses to send me to my room for punishment. All were blatant excuses for him to come to my bedroom and find reasons to violate my innocence. He eventually no longer allowed me to keep my blouse or shirt on when he examined me and stripped me to the waist. My saying that I lived in constant fear and anguish as a child in their home would not adequately express what I felt living with them.

Several times, I attempted to get my mother to do something to help me, but she wouldn't. I ran away; they brought me back. I was punished worse for running away. They owned me. The exams got more and more intrusive until one time—just one time—he made me take my pants down. He came into my bedroom at night, and no cries for help brought me any mother who cared. I turned him in the next day to the school nurse. I had a lot to think about. My reasoning became, *I know if I turn him in, I'm going to lose my mother too.* For a twelve-year-old girl, it was a hard choice. *And if I turn him in, and they make me stay like they did Sarra, the abuse will get worse. If I just run away and don't turn him in, I will get beat if they find me. I've already lost my real father, am I ready to lose my mother too?*

All these thoughts plagued me. But I knew I had to pay the cost of giving up my mother. I so wanted her. I so wanted her to be normal and loving and a safe place to be, but the truth was, she wasn't any of those.

She was charmed like a cobra snake and could bite as badly as he did. Whether I liked that truth or not, I had to give her up. So I did. The cost not to was too high, and I wasn't going to pay it. I reported his abuse to the school nurse. I was sent to the local hospital for a real doctor's checkup, lots of processing and people and legalities. I was too young to understand it all. I never went home after school that day or for weeks that followed. It was late May and close to school ending for the summer. The town I would have to go to foster care in was not in our school district, so a family from our district took me in to stay with them for two weeks. During those two weeks, I learned that I won an award for Student of the Year. I was given a medal onstage, and I again wished my mother believed in me and would be present. But of course, I was on my own; there would be no parent present. I started feeling my heart harden to life.

A few weeks passed, and school ended. I had to go with a social worker and a caseworker to Merlin and Dorothy's house to get my clothes and move to the new foster home. It was the first time facing either of them since I reported the abuse to the school. The social worker was taken in by Merlin's charm. We sat in the living room of the house; a cardboard box sat ready and packed with my clothes and some personal items. The atmosphere was creepy. Merlin was so sugary and so syrupy to the social worker. I could not believe how she was being taken in by his lies. I sat in silence. I was being treated like the bad child who had behavior problems and wouldn't mind, who ran away because she was such a bad girl. I said nothing. My mother didn't say a word, didn't stick up for me, and didn't defend me. She sat silently on the couch next to Merlin, hands in her lap—not a tear shed. When we left the house and formalities of good-bye were passed, I sat in the front seat between the social worker and the caseworker.

The charmed social worker started in, "Well, what do you feel?"

"I don't want to talk about it."

"Do you feel like crying? It's okay if you do," she continued on.

I went inside myself and never said a word, but I thought, *I feel like you shutting up and leaving me alone. And I feel like if my mother can't shed a tear for me, I'm not crying for her, not now, not ever.*

And at that moment, in that second of time, I grew rebellious, and my heart completed the hardening it had started. I was a different girl—a girl I didn't like or love; a girl who didn't know how to be loved; a young girl who looked for love in all the wrong places, not realizing being used and needed wasn't real love.

Only Brian—the boy who cared enough to drive to the foster home to see if I was okay, the boy who always saw something under the hardened heart and the pain of a young girl's soul—only Brian could ever reach me emotionally, going past the walls of rebellion that I built to protect myself. I adopted a heart for the underdog, for the person who seemed unable to fend for themselves, for the person that society seemed to reject. I refused to go along with the norm.

I thought it odd that teachers couldn't understand why young girls who had been sexually abused were more promiscuous than other "normal" girls their age. Some teachers judge the way you look, act, flirt, and respond to boys. One teacher even went so far as to having me stand in the paper wastebasket next to his desk because he caught me passing a note that was a game of questions. One of the questions asked was, "Have you ever kissed a boy in your pajamas?" The truth was, I didn't remember ever kissing a boy in my pajamas, but I circled the *yes* and not the *no*.

Mr. Davis took the note, read it, and made me go to the front of the room, where he made me stand in the wastebasket and said, "You're where you belong, white trash, for answering affirmative to such questions! Only trash would answer affirmative to kissing a boy in her pajamas!"

The principal got involved, and I was in trouble for addressing Mr. Davis as *he* instead of as *Mr. Davis*, while trying to explain the whole ordeal. But here's the answer to a little girl's violated innocence. After a dirty old man touches you and you have no say about it—about the violation of the whole embarrassing, humiliating, scary experience—there's a sense of freedom in the fact that a young boy your age that you choose finds you appealing and wants to touch you; it was that simple. Their touch could bring a sense that you were wanted or loved. Being rejected by your parents can cause it. Is it right? No, it isn't. But until there is an inner healing, young rejected, violated girls are walking around, wounded and broken, looking for someone to care and love them.

Brian saw through all that. He didn't have to touch me; he just loved me and cared for me just like I was. He seemed to understand how difficult it was for me to live with a family I didn't know and try to "fit in." My foster parents were wonderful people. A young couple with four children, I watched the children for them during the summer while they worked their day jobs. It was a nice summer job, and I made some spending money. The children were great kids, and I learned to love them quickly. I was safe there. I started school in a new school system. I had good grades, enjoyed learning, and after school, especially enjoyed going to my own bedroom in the foster home and not being afraid.

After six months, the social service system wanted "reunification," and I had to go back to my stepfather and mother—on what I didn't know was a final visit of the social worker to my foster parents' home. It became clear to my foster parents and to me that the social worker was taken in by Merlin. There was a meeting with Merlin, Dorothy, the social worker, the caseworker, my foster parents, and myself present. The social worker stated in front of my foster parents that maybe I "was not understanding Merlin, that could it be possible I was just jealous of him and my mother, that when he comes home from working hard on the railroad, my mother gives him attention and I'm jealous of that attention."

Merlin sat all smug. He thought he won the battle. He had been working on her since the May before, when I was taken out of his house. Yet my foster father saw right through his lies and diabolical ways. He stood up, demanded an apology for me, and told that social worker off but good! He added that she too owed me an apology and swiftly directed them all to get out of his house. Within days, without notice, the social worker picked me up in the middle of a school day, took me back to my foster parents to pack my clothes and say good-bye, then dropped me off at Merlin and Dorothy's—never to be seen again. I was back. He won. I lived in fear.

It wasn't many months later when Merlin and Dorothy decided to move out of the State of Pennsylvania to New York State. They asked my brother Gandy to leave the farm and required him to move out of state with us. It was December of Gandy's senior year in high school. He reluctantly agreed to leave his farm family and his work there, departing with great sadness. My mother took me aside and gave me this notice, "If Merlin becomes a problem for you, don't go to the social services again, just get out and find a place to live."

I actually was relieved to have her tell me that, because it would be exactly what I would do. Gandy's departure came quicker than mine. It happened during the move. Gandy had worked like a mule, lugging and moving furniture and boxes, with Merlin bossing Dorothy and Gandy in every step they made as they loaded the truck.

Dorothy had an old-fashioned loom, which had to be disassembled to be moved. Gandy did the whole process himself, exhausted as the day grew longer, and the packing and moving went on into the evening. The trip back to New York from the house in Pennsylvania would take a couple of hours. Gandy was already overly tired. The roads were snowy. The weather was cold and snowy, making visibility difficult. By the time we made the long haul back to the New York house, every nerve of every person was at its peak. Unloading the truck, Gandy went to sit down and rest. Merlin was having none of that; he rode and rode Gandy, pushing and pushing him to the place of sheer exhaustion.

Gandy kept working. Merlin sat and gave orders.

When the truck was unloaded, Merlin asked, "Where're the screws to the loom?"

No one knew. No one could find them. Then Dorothy remembered seeing them. "I saw them in an old coffee can in the loom room. They must still be there."

Merlin started in, addressing his comments to Gandy, "If you weren't so damn stupid, you would have grabbed that can. How the hell can we put the loom together without those screws?"

That pushed Gandy's exhausted body over the edge. Gandy yelled, "And if you weren't so damn lazy and would get up and help with something, maybe we'd have them!"

That was it! All hell broke loose right there, right that minute. Merlin grabbed the handle of a mop and started beating Gandy with it. Gandy ran and ended up in an adjacent room, where I was standing.

Merlin took the handle of that mop and with both hands shoved it up against Gandy's throat, pinning him to the wall. Gandy's color compromised.

I started yelling, "Mom, stop him, stop him, he's gonna kill Gandy!"

Mom must have seen it too because she started pulling on Merlin's shoulder.

Merlin, in his rage, turned around and pushed her; and when he did, it released Gandy. The next thing I knew, Gandy was leaving.

"I'm not coming back!"

He was gone after the explosion, and Merlin was bitching at Dorothy, accusing her of "taking sides against him."

Gandy called Becca, who drove the two hours to pick him up out of the cold, snowy night. He went to live on the farm with the old couple who loved him. My brother was gone for good. I was glad for him. He would be back in Starrucca, back on the farm with an old couple who loved him, needed him, and appreciated him. He would be back with his best friend, Brian, able to finish his senior year in his own high school—not a new school, where he didn't know anyone. No, he was gone, but I knew he was better off, just like Benn, Becca, and Sarra—gone and finally free.

By the end of that school year, Merlin attempted once again to threaten me with his sexual advances.

I no longer believed I had to put up with his sickness. I told Mom he threatened me, and she said, "I told you to just go find someplace to live."

So I did. I went to school with a girl whose father allowed me to come and stay with them. She and her cousin were two of my best friends in school, Roxanne and Debbie—to this day, in our sixties, we are still knit together by the bonds of friendship, though we live miles apart. I stayed with Roxanne. She shared her room with me and never complained.

She knew I loved to sing, and at night, she would say, "Mary Pat, sing us to sleep."

Roxy somehow understood my pain and loneliness as her heart was hurting too. Her mother had died of cancer only months before my moving in with her family. During the time of my living there in my friend's home, Brian came and visited me, though it was two hours from his home in Starucca. He was always such a relief in my chaotic, mixed-up life. It was during that season that we became more than serious friends. His intention was to go in the Army after his graduation, and when he finished, we would be married. Little did I know then that Vietnam would change our plan and the Vietnam War would affect my life forever. Though I was never there in the war, the war helped define me.

I stayed with Roxanne until September of my senior year. It was September 1970. My mother came to the house and asked me if I wanted to come and live with her and Merlin.

She said there was talk around town and that I should just come home. I had no idea what point she was trying to make, but I figured she asked, and so she must have wanted me there. So I went "home." I was only there three weeks when my sister Sarra's call came that Brian had been killed in Vietnam.

CHAPTER 12

I HAD BEEN BACK IN Dorothy and Merlin's home such a short time when the phone call came that changed my life. After the initial shock of hearing Brian was dead, I had a week before the next call came, telling me his body was back in the USA and his viewing for the family was going to be the "next day."

It all seemed so unreal to me—like a stranger in my mother and stepfather's home. I lay in my bed the night before his funeral and dreaded the reality of it all. I couldn't accept not seeing Brian move, lying still and unresponsive. I couldn't handle that he was not alive. I was crying and trying to keep my sobs suppressed from my stepfather and mother. I didn't want them to hear me downstairs as I lay in my bedroom upstairs, heart wrenched in my room. My mind flooded with thoughts.

In my brokenness and emotional pain, I started crying out, asking, "Why do some children's lives seem so happy and normal, like the cheerleaders', and others were so broken by life with things—like what Roxanne had to go through losing her mom to cancer or mine who watched all my sisters and brothers abuse? How could that be? Is there a God?" I felt like asking Him, "God, are you there really?" And then I thought, *If there wasn't a God, would it be okay for me to go wherever Brian was?* So I said, "It isn't like I want to die, but I just don't know how to live. Would it be okay for me to go wherever he is? Like if this is life and this is what the world is like, why can't I leave earth too?"

All these thoughts raced through my mind as I lay crying in my bedroom alone. Then all of a sudden, something happened that would change my life more profoundly than anything—including the war and the death of Brian—ever had. In my crying out, seeking "Is there a God" and "Are you real?" a presence filled my room. Something *very* tall and very peaceful stood by my bed and brought a calm with it. I say *it* because I did not know if it was male or female. I only knew it had a form, as we do, but was much bigger and taller than we are.

It looked at me, and without moving its mouth but just by its eyes, I heard, "Jesus has a reason for you."

Then as swiftly as it came, it was gone. I had total peace. I no longer was crying. I no longer felt the need to leave earth. I knew, though—as painful as Brian's loss was—that I could live and that I had a reason to be here. Whatever that reason was, it had something to do with the name of Jesus. I was changed. I came to believe that we are not just a body, but we are soul and spirit. When we leave the earth, it is not over for us. A part of us lives on, and that has something to do with Jesus. I did not immediately understand it all then, nor do I now. I was exposed to a truth, and truth would lead my journey, eventually bringing wisdom into my life and giving me a personal relationship with my Creator.

I went the next day to see Brian in a coffin, not moving, not responding. When I walked into the funeral parlor, I recalled every detail of the dream I had in the foster home—of the vivid flowers around the casket, the sconces on the wall, the dim pink light, except now I knew what I didn't know then. It was Brian.

Brian was honored with a military funeral: a twelve-gun salute, the playing of taps in the graveyard, the honor of the folding of his flag. It didn't make it easier, but it did matter that he was recognized for living a life that proved he gave his for others, including mine. Brian's life came to be an influential part of my life. His being on the earth allowed a messenger to tell me that I have purpose and meaning. It isn't every day that an angel shows up to tell you that God is real! Knowing that truth—and that the truth is in Jesus—I was able to handle whatever was behind me and whatever would be ahead for me in life.

Life went on. The village of Starrucca, my memories with Brian, life with my siblings, my childhood—all was behind me. I graduated high school and made plans to attend community college. But before any of that came to fruition, my stepfather, Merlin, had to have one more "last word."

I was seventeen, had just finished my senior year. It was 1971. Merlin decided he didn't want me living with him and my mother anymore. No explanation. He just said, "Get on your bicycle and ride, kid." I was made to leave their home. I packed my belongings and walked away.

Mom stood and watched as I closed the door behind me. No words were exchanged. From age seventeen to age twenty-two, he would not allow me to see my mother or to have contact with her, nor did she try.

The days following Brian's funeral melted one day into another. I worked as a waitress in the local ice cream shop in town, saving my money for college. I babysat for some wonderful people, Dyke and Zilla Cook. They had one little girl, Renaye, who was two years old and the sunshine in their lives. She came to be sunshine in my life too. I enjoyed watching her and spending time with her, watching her grow and cherishing what it was really like when parents loved their child. I saved my babysitting money and my waitress money, hoping to use it toward school after graduation.

One day, when I was leaving work, Gene Cook—Dyke's brother—pulled up in his yellow Z28 Camaro. He pulled to the curb near the sidewalk where I was walking.

"Hey, I heard what happened to your boyfriend. I'm really sorry. Want to hang out and go for a ride?"

I didn't really know him. I had seen him once when I was a junior, and he came to a basketball game at our school. He graduated in 1968, so he typically wasn't around. He had joined the Marines and did his tours in Vietnam. The night a friend of mine (Johnny) introduced Gene to me on the bleachers at the game, he was on crutches from the war. I remembered clearly seeing a curly-headed little girl's face around him when I met him. I thought it was strange. I didn't know what it meant, and I never questioned my imaginings. I just lived, knowing there was something special about him to me. So when he pulled up to that curb years later, I was grateful he did, because I was lonely and lost in a world much bigger than me.

I got in the car without reserve. Gene didn't say much. He cranked the music. James Taylor's *Sweet Baby James* album played, and we rode and rode and rode—like a magic-carpet ride—away from the world and any weight of its pain. Those rides became common relief for Gene and me. He didn't talk much; he drove. It was music cranked and rides through the mountains, past cornfields and farmhouses, trees and homes, where people inside felt normal and we, as watchers, rode. We would stop at the creeks and the fields.

One day Gene really opened up to me. He told me his life story, including the reality that at age fifteen, he lost his mother to cancer. Six months later, his father died of a heart attack. Gene felt his dad died of a broken heart, really. He said his dad missed his mom so much that he was not the same after her death. After his Dad died, Gene went into a foster situation with an aunt and uncle until his brother, Dyke, and sister-in-law, Zilla, could take him in when his brother turned twenty-one. As soon as Gene graduated, he joined the Marines. He was wounded in Vietnam; that was why he was on crutches years before when I met him at the basketball game. He was home on a medical leave from the Marines. He was deeply affected from the war's atrocities and its horrendous killings. He had severe post-traumatic stress disorder, but at the time, neither he—nor I— knew how deeply the trauma of the war was in him.

Gene introduced me to weed, and I smoked it when he asked because I thought to myself, *Who really cares if I do or I don't.* So I did. But I decided early in life, I didn't want to do drugs, because I wanted children one day, and I didn't want my body messed up, somehow messing them up. So I didn't become much of a companion who could share Gene's world, except for those rides that kept us bonded.

One day Gene stopped the car along a stream. We walked into the woods and sat by the water that rippled over the rocks. The summer air was warm; the shade of the hemlocks along the creek was inviting. We hung our feet over the edge of some huge natural boulders, dangling our feet in the water below.

Gene asked, "You have anything in your purse to eat?"

I dug in my bag. "Yeah, not much, but some crackers."

The crinkle of the paper and a few crumbs later, Gene said, "Give me your foot. Watch." He placed the bits of crackers between my toes. "Now, put your foot in the water."

When I did—within seconds—tiny, little minnows were nibbling at the crackers, tickling my feet. The water was so cool and the little fish so clear to see. It was one of the most innocent feelings I have ever had. I sat beside that cool stream many times in my mind's eye when the world got too fast and Gene got too far away.

He and I formed a comfortable bond during those months. It felt like we had fallen in love with each other. It went without saying. Vietnam was a common thread for us. We didn't need a lot of words. We had our music of the '60s and our Z-28 Camaro rides. Then one day, as quickly as he came into my life, he was gone. I went to work to babysit his niece, Renaye, and his sister-in-law told me Gene had left for California. He never said a word to me about it. He was just gone. The day before, we were grilling steaks at the stone trestle, and Gene decided to tell me that he loved me, out of the blue, "I really dig ya, Kel. I love ya."

I knew that was a lot for him to admit. He had walls, and no one was supposed to see past them. But I did, and now he was gone. Gene had filled a huge void in my life. I really had no one nearby, no family. My mother was off-limits, and all my siblings lived far away. Dyke and Zilla and their little girl filled an empty space in my heart. I loved being with them and being in their home. They were good people, and they were good to me. I finished my summer work and moved into a house in Corning with five other girls who were attending college. I became very close to my roommate, Sophia. I was glad, of all the girls that were in the house, that she was the one I shared my room with. We were quite different in many ways, but I appreciated the artist in her. She helped me see what I would have missed seeing—art—through her eyes. Sophia was raised in a liberal, sophisticated environment. It appeared her parents cherished that she was the only girl with a handful of brothers. She was a gifted girl. I thought she looked like something out of a magazine. It always felt like I needed to protect her somehow. She even married one of my best friends. It was good to have her in my life. I had a void from Gene being gone, and it seemed a friendship helped soften that. I really missed him and our rides through the hills.

My money soon ran out; I couldn't pay rent. I had trouble focusing on my classes. I tried to find work and couldn't, and it just seemed like I was making bad choices and getting nowhere in life. I was sad and lonely and broken. The truth is, I wasn't even aware of how broken I really was. I looked for love in all the wrong places. I turned cold. I had a month of the semester left when a letter came, out of the blue, from Gene. He said he was coming back from California, that he loved me and if I would want to move in together.

So December 10, Gene picked me up at the house I had shared with the girls at college in a car with a water bed strapped to its roof, and off we rode into our lives of emotional need that neither one of us could truly fill for one another, though we would try. We moved back to the town we graduated from. Gene rented a trailer from his uncle, and I moved in with him. I had no money; he had a little. I found a job in a factory thirty miles from town, rode there every weekday with a car full of older ladies, and contributed to the gas for the ride to work. It was not what I pictured for my life, but here I was in a groove, where having someone to love and be there for me was more important than common sense.

Because common sense would have finished college, not turned my paycheck over to my boyfriend, who spent his days at the town pool hall and local bar. Maybe he would be home when I got home, and maybe he wouldn't be. Yet I was convinced he loved me, or he would have never come from California to get me. That's all I needed—him. We were both so wounded by Vietnam we had no idea how much. I was sure I could fill all his hurts and needs; I was sure I could change him into a stable partner to share life. Finally, we would both have someone. We didn't have to be watchers anymore; we could be joiners.

But that's not what happened. I'm not saying anything bad about him; we both made mistakes. We just didn't make it. Our pain was too deep and too much a part of who we were we didn't stand a chance.

Yet one of the most beautiful blessings came out of our lives. We married and had a beautiful baby girl: a dark- and curly-headed eight-pound-twelve-ounce little bundle of love, real love. I was twenty-one years old, and on June 27, 1975, she entered our world and captured our hearts—Arika Kelly Cook.

It was May of 1974, the year before Arika was born, that I had an experience with God that changed my life. I was disillusioned with life and the reality of it. I thought marriage would have filled the void I had. It didn't. It caused me to want to know what the angel meant when the messenger said, "Jesus has a reason for you." Somehow that had to mean there was more to this than what I had lived so far. I believed there was something more, and I was missing it. I started seeking God, asking questions about life and Him. I got a Bible because I felt as if He was telling me that my answers were in there. I didn't go to a special church or join a special religion. I just sought God and His Spirit. I could feel Him. I knew He was near, and I knew somehow Jesus had something to do with all this. I started wanting to stay out of the local bar and instead read my Bible. I didn't want to be at the parties anymore or around people that were smoking pot. I wanted to be by the river in front of our cabin and watch the stars and breathe fresh air and hear music that touched my soul, not disrupted it. I couldn't understand a lot of what I was reading in the Bible; it didn't make sense to me.

It seemed like one king was killing another king and there were wars going on, and I didn't get it. Yet I still felt like God was telling me, "Just keep reading, your answers are there." So I kept reading. I read every chance I got. Then one night, when working the four-to-midnight shift, I was on a break, walking toward the women's lounge to sit and read my Bible on my lunch break. The security guard got up from his desk as he saw me walking toward him and toward the door to the lounge. He had a look on his face that I couldn't explain.

I didn't know if I was in trouble for bringing my Bible into work or having it in a public place or what.

He approached me, "What are you reading?"

My thoughts were defensive. I wondered why he was asking me. I didn't care if there was any problem; I was going to tell him the truth.

"My Bible," I said.

He looked intense, "Why are you reading that?"

The look on his face was now serious. I decided I didn't care if he thought I was odd or crazy or even if he had a problem with me having a Bible at work. It was my break. I wasn't doing anything wrong, and I had a half hour free to read. I looked him square in the eyes and responded, "Well, you may not believe this, but I feel like God is trying to tell me something, that the answers to my questions are in here."

That guard, as seriously as I had ever seen anyone, looked at me and said, "He is. He *is* trying to tell you something." Then he said to me, "Have you ever asked Jesus to be your Lord and Savior?"

Puzzled, I studied him and said, "Well, I think I have. I mean, I believe in Him, and I talk to Him."

Quickly he stated, "No, when you're loved by Jesus, you don't 'think' you are, you 'know' you are." He continued, "Would you want to ask Jesus into your heart to be your Lord and Savior tonight? I'll pray with you."

I looked away, scanning my eyes over all the machines and the people at them, wondering what was happening to me. What would these people say, seeing me here, praying with the guard? Then I immediately realized, it didn't matter what they said or what they thought or what anyone thought. They didn't live my life; I did. I didn't want to miss it.

With great expectation, I quickly added, "Yes, yes, I'll pray with you! Yes, I want Jesus to be my Lord. I believe in Him!"

We bowed our heads, and the guard proceeded to lead me in prayer and told me to repeat after him these words:

"God, I believe in You. I believe You died on the cross for my sin and shame and that You rose again on the third day and now You are seated in heaven. I am asking You to forgive my sin and come into my heart, Jesus. I love You and want to live my life for You."

It was a short and heartfelt prayer of faith and repentance, but I felt every breath of it. I heard these words: "I will never leave you nor forsake you."

I was so taken back by hearing these words. I looked up into the huge pipes and ducts in the ceiling of the factory. I thought they must have come from there. But they didn't; they came from God Himself, speaking to me personally. I was so affected. I had never heard of such a thing!

The guard later shared this with me. He told me that typically, he worked only the day shift and that he hadn't worked overtime in years but that the Lord had spoken to Him and told him to work overtime because someone was "coming into the kingdom tonight," and he would be praying with that person. He told me that God showed him when I was walking down the aisle toward the lounge and the guard desk, that I was the person "coming home." Tears of gratitude and joy filled my being. I *knew* I was loved.

Accepting Jesus as my Lord only seemed to build a bigger chasm between Gene and me. We were attracted to different things and different people. But what we had in common was our history—Vietnam's pain; our love, no matter how it was defined; and our sweet child, Arika, who made all the difference. I stayed in faith, and it seemed I loved Gene even more because with Christ, it appeared I understood his brokenness.

Somehow, though, Gene was getting farther and farther from me. But God was faithful, and truly, He never left me or forsook me. I studied my Bible every spare minute. I didn't join a particular church at first, though I tried several churches in town. Whatever happened to me that night that I accepted Jesus as my Lord in the factory was not happening in the churches. They were missing something, but I didn't know how to explain that—until I met a college intern who had come to work that summer in the factory.

When she saw how excited I was over my newfound freedom in Christ, she told me that there was an older lady who had a log cabin on the mountain that held Bible studies in her home every Tuesday night and invited me to go. I went. From that first Tuesday night on, I went for years following every Tuesday night. I studied the Word of God. I was baptized. I received the baptism of the Holy Spirit, and I lived a willing life of surrender to God. He showed Himself faithful to me over and over again. He heard my heart and always responded to my love for Him. I learned that's what life is about—a love relationship with Jesus. As He said, "A new commandment I give unto you, that you love one another as I have loved you. By this shall all men know that you are my disciple, if you have love one for another" (John, KJV). I absolutely knew He loved me, and I absolutely loved Him.

One day, when I was on my knees, crying in our bedroom by our bed because Arika needed shoes and had outgrown what shoes she had (we had no income except for my forty-seven-dollar-a-week unemployment check, which bought our groceries and diapers), I cried out to God, "Lord, I know I've made mistakes. I know I'm in this situation because I chose this marriage, but my daughter needs shoes, and I feel guilty that I can't get her any. Please help me get her shoes."

No one knew I prayed that prayer alone with God, no one.

But that night, I rode a school bus to an evangelistic meeting out of town. When I entered the sanctuary, I stayed in the back of the church.

A woman I didn't know walked up to me with a bag in her hand, and she said to me, "The Lord told me to give these to you."

I thanked her, and we joined in the service. At the end of the meeting, on the bus ride home, I looked in the bag. There were baby clothes, lots of them, just Arika's size. But at the very bottom of the bag, in a little shoebox, was a perfect little pair of shoes for my baby. He was always faithful. He saw my heart.

Gene eventually came around. He started loving God. He saw something in me, and he said he wanted it too. For a few years, we walked in Holy Spirit together. But it didn't last; the world had a stronghold, and there were strongholds that needed to be broken in both of our lives. The prince of the power of the air wasn't giving up that easy on us. He wasn't letting us go and was gearing up for the battle of our lives. Yet in the midst of our dysfunction, we had a miracle. It's a testimony of the faithfulness of God and my faith in a God Who loves us and created us for a relationship with Him. You don't have to be perfect to be loved by Jesus; neither do you have to be perfect to have miracles happen in your life. In fact, it's the contrite and broken heart He reaches for. It's the humble of heart that's the real deal.

This is what I've learned. What I am going to share with you is as it happened. These words have been within me, waiting to be written. If you need love, healing, or a miracle in your life, please don't let these words escape you. Regardless of what you do with the rest of my book, absorb this next chapter, and know that Jesus is Lord and He never leaves us and His love is always available to us. We just need to draw close to Him. The Holy Spirit, the Holy Ghost of God, moves on our behalf as He moved upon the face of the deep over the water when He created us for a relationship with Him. He is the Infinite and allows us to align ourselves with the infinite. He still moves in our lives today, and He is greater than any adversity, trial, negative people, or death that tries to come against us. We can hear His voice and follow Him, aligning ourselves with His will, His purpose, His plan. His salvation is a gift of God, not of works, lest anyone think their works cause them to be righteous. In fact, self-righteous people grieve and bruise me.

Religious people have almost destroyed me more than once. God's love is greater, though, than to let religion rob a personal relationship with Him. We are righteous through the blood of Jesus and what He did for us, nothing more. He bought us back from lust that sold us out to the prince of the power of the air, the devil. Yes, there is a devil, just like there is a God. It's a universe bigger than you or me. I admit I do not understand it all, but I know some truth that has been a code to live by on my journey. I've seen it work. I've seen God be personal, and I know He found me. All He asks us to do is love Him back then seek, search, and save the lost for Him too, never losing the simplicity of Jesus's love.

I have learned how to think analytically and supernaturally. Both are relevant in life's journey. You're part of two kingdoms, the flesh and the spirit. We are given the privilege of living in both if we choose.

 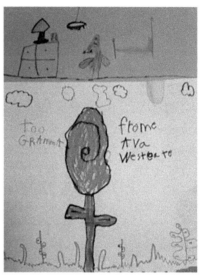

CHAPTER 13

IT BEGAN WITH HER STEPS. Arika Kelly Cook—my daughter of nine months old—walked perfectly well with strong, stable strides and a newfound freedom of liberation in every step. It was a pleasure experiencing her joy as her little feet pattered across the floor, exploring every new inch of our home.

But within a few months, that all changed, first evidenced by slight behavioral changes. For instance, during her playtime, after waking from her nap, she would easily fall asleep, right in the middle of her toys! That seemed concerning to me. How could she be tired? She just woke up half an hour ago. Then instead of just wetting a diaper, she would be soaked, saturated, neckline-to-ankles wet, and frequently, her little "onesies" being changed continuously throughout the day, wetting head to toe. She started having less bowel movement, and when she did go, it appeared to be a strain on her.

As a new mother and Arika being a first child, I wondered what was normal development and what wasn't. These changes were magnified for me. She wasn't crying; she wasn't fussy; she just appeared to be going through some changes. They were never consistent—rather, sporadic. She could be fine one day with no exaggerated wetting, staying awake, playing for hours, and moving her bowels as easily as any other child would; then the next day appear in stress, straining with fear in her eyes, as she gazed into mine—a silent cry that screamed to me, "Help me, Mommy."

I was working the midnight-to-eight shift in the factory. I had given Arika her nightly bath, put her in her jammies, and laid her in her crib. I stayed by her, singing a low, sweet lullaby of praise—like I did most nights if she wasn't already asleep when I placed her in her crib. I would sing the Word of God over her, or songs I had learned in worship at the church. She responded to the presence the praise brought and would sweetly, gently fall off to sleep.

This night was different after she fell asleep. I heard the Lord speak to me, giving me instruction, "You won't be going into work tonight, call off."

It startled me a bit, but I was clear that it was His direction. So I called my employer and told them, "I will not be coming into work tonight."

Giving advance notice ahead and not making a habit of missing work made my call off work no problem. Then, since I wasn't going to work, I too could lay down and rest, so I did. Hours later, I was awakened in the middle of the night by Arika's whimpers. I immediately went to her crib side and picked her up, grateful that I was there for her, as she felt extremely warm and she was obviously very uncomfortable and not feeling well. I attempted to bring her fever down and to comfort her belly, but nothing seemed to soothe her. Within minutes, I knew I was home not by chance but by divine appointment. I was taking her to the emergency room at our local hospital. It was 2:00 a.m. I completed admission paperwork as the medical staff took Arika to run some tests. By 4:00 a.m., I had a report from the on-call doctor. He stated that Arika had an X-ray to her chest and that she had pneumonia. He told me she was running a fever of 104 from this and that they were able to bring her fever down. They gave me amoxicillin and phenobarbital for spiked fevers, instructed me to give her cool baths to keep her comfortable, and told me to make an appointment and see her pediatrician Monday for a follow-up.

We left the hospital. I had absolutely no peace. I live by the Word that says, "Let the peace of God *rule* your heart." No peace was there. How could this be pneumonia? She hadn't a cough. She had no runny nose. She showed no sign of congestion prior, or now. Pneumonia? It made no sense to me. I gave her the amoxicillin as prescribed. Then her smooth, soft, fresh baby skin had broken out in little red bumps, and so I called the twenty-four-hour line and reported this. I was advised that Arika must be reacting to the amoxicillin, and since I had an appointment Monday, hold off on giving it to her and the doctor would see her Monday. I was able to keep her fevers at bay over that weekend, and I was grateful for that.

Still I had no peace that this was pneumonia. Something else was at work here in my daughter's body. I knew it, but I didn't know what—not yet, anyway. Monday, I took Arika in to see her pediatrician. I expressed my concern to him, that I don't think this was pneumonia.

The doctor walked to his bookshelf and pointed to his books and said, "You are just the mother, I am the doctor. She has on the X-ray shown pneumonia in her lung." He was upset with me.

I was embarrassed, angry, and still not convinced; something else was at work here. I could feel it—yes, because I am the mother. He sent us both home with a new prescription to replace the amoxicillin, as it was reported she was showing an allergic reaction to it. And my instruction was, "to calm down and she was going to be just fine." So I did what he said. I took her home. I still had not reported back to work. I could not leave her. They could have fired me, but I could not leave her. She would lie in my arms for hours at a time. I poured my spirit into her. I kept her fever from spiking, and I could feel that my presence comforted my baby. I called the doctor again because when Arika would walk even short distances between the couch and the chair, she would fall.

He assured me she was just tired from having been sick. It was clear to me that she was fighting something and in a great struggle. She would not fight this alone. At my Tuesday night Bible study, I requested prayer for her, explaining that it was troubling not having clarity on what was going on with her. I also shared the information the doctor gave me that this was pneumonia. However, my prayers were against something not yet defined, something robbing my child. She appeared to be getting weaker by the day.

I called the doctor again and reported that Arika seemed to be hurting in her feet—that when I would put her down from holding her, as soon as her feet touched the floor, she drew her legs up to her belly and wouldn't let me put her down. He reluctantly told me to bring her in tomorrow for an appointment.

It seemed to me that he thought, "that mother" was at it again, in his book!

It was Wednesday. I kept the appointment for her, carrying her into the doctor's office. He instructed me to put her down. When I did, he saw her response. She cried and drew her legs up. She appeared weaker and weaker to me; her body was losing the strength it used to hold. Limpness was coming over her.

Immediately, when he saw what her response was to having her feet touch the floor, he reported, "I'm going to admit her in the hospital. We need to do some more tests."

Relieved yet still troubled over whatever was happening to her, at least now I felt like we would get to the bottom of it. He didn't apologize. The hospital was next door to the doctor's office. I walked over, carrying Arika. They admitted her and started some tests. It was still Wednesday. By Wednesday night, she had been poked, prodded, examined, tested, and had evidence of it by several tiny needle marks that had been placed in her spine, checking her protein count, and in her arms, where blood was drawn. My baby girl—eleven months old, just short of her first birthday—here in this hospital, appearing listless and dazed, drifting farther from me. I could feel it. I could feel her slipping.

Still there were no reports of what actually was wrong with my child or what was happening to her.

Thursday came. An experience on Thursday in that hospital about put me over the edge. Lunchtime, my daughter was being fed in a high chair by a nurse. I walked into the room, and there was my little girl slumped over as far to the right as the high chair would allow her to go without falling out of the chair sideways. She could not sit up! She had no ability, no strength to support herself, no ability to sit up at all! The nurse was placing baby food on a spoon and continued feeding her, as if this position was normal. Arika was not interested in eating and resisted the spoonfuls of pabulum. I totally lost it!

"Can't you see she can't sit up? She doesn't want that right now! What is going on here?" I shouted! "Stop, get her out of that chair right now!"

Arika was relieved I was there. I had seen the strain on her face even as the baby food was being shoved in her mouth. I was furious. I picked my child up and held her ... and held her ... and held her. She was too exhausted to do anything but lie limp against me. There were no tests done Thursday. I spent the day in her hospital room, holding her close to me, afraid she would slip from me if I put her down. Friday came. The doctor showed up for his routine morning rounds.

"Doctor, I want my child moved to a medical center where they can tell me what is going on with her, why she can't even sit up anymore, why she has no movement in her body."

"Now, now, we are running tests that will show us what is physically happening to her. We will have answers soon."

"Running tests? You haven't done any tests since Wednesday when she was admitted. She's lying here, losing her ability to live. I want her moved!"

"We have scheduled extensive X-rays for her today. We will have answers for you this afternoon on completion of those X-rays. I can't stop you if you choose to move her to a medical center, but it's premature. Let us just do these X-rays, and we will know more."

I cautiously agreed to allow the X-rays instead of stubbornly moving her to a medical center, fully expecting that at least the X-rays would give us some answers now. Friday afternoon, they wheeled her down to the X-ray department. I waited and I waited. They wheeled her back up. I waited and I waited. When would the report come? When would I have some answers? It was after 5:00 p.m. now. The hospital staff had changed shifts; the lab and other departments were closing. Where were the results of her tests?

Why wasn't I given any results? Arika was worse; she seemed almost unconscious to me, lying limp.

Life was draining out of her, seeping slowly minute by minute, hour by hour, day by day. Where was the doctor? Where were the answers to her tests and X-rays? Why wasn't someone doing something? I asked the floor nurse about her X-rays. Her response was that no tests or X-rays had been sent up to the floor. She had no answers for me. It was Friday night. The doctor had gone home. I had no report, no answers, no feedback from the time they had wheeled her away from me. What did they do? Did they even take X-rays as the doctor claimed he had ordered? The night was long, and Arika was further away than ever. I was scared. I was terribly afraid of what I was seeing. I held her and kept my life in her. I couldn't let her pass. She must stay with me; she had to stay with me.

"Don't go, Arika, don't go," I would whisper to her, "I can't live without you, don't leave, stay with me," as I held her limp little baby body in my arms, desperate not to let her slip away.

I spoke the Word of God into her. I sang softly words of life over her. I became the barrier between death and my daughter. Though that dark night was long and morning seemed forever away, I would not let death swallow her up. Morning came, and with it the doctor on his routine rounds again. This was it. Boldly, I attacked, like a mother bear protecting her cub.

"Where are the reports you said I would have concerning the results of Arika's X-rays yesterday? I am tired of the procrastination and the delay that leaves me with no answers. I want my daughter moved!"

The doctor seemed as surprised as I was angry!

"What do you mean you were not given the results of the X-rays?"

"Just what I said, I haven't been told anything! I'm watching my daughter fade in front of my face, and nothing, nothing, is happening here to slow this down!"

He showed immediate concern. He could see Arika had become much worse and that I truly had not been given any report. He excused himself went into the hall, and I heard with a very loud voice the discussion that took place outside of that hospital room. The next thing I knew, staff was in emergency mode. A light code was given (I can't remember what color it was). I only know that the code caused a lot of action on Arika's behalf. Because what had happened was that the X-rays had definitely been taken and left downstairs, having not been read. When they were read it, it was proven to be extremely serious.

"There is a mass on your daughter's spine. We must get her to Strong Memorial Hospital in Rochester as soon as possible."

He made it very clear he was sorry and that there was an urgency in getting her to Rochester. He wanted to transport her by ambulance, but I wanted her to go up with her father and me. It was a two-hour drive. I wasn't leaving her.

The ride in our Volkswagen bug with our little girl strapped in her car seat seemed like a dream—as if life stopped and the time we were in the car together was like a gift of time given to us all to reflect on.

Like some scene from the play *Our Town*, we were all embracing every sacred minute, every sacred mile, every sacred breath—knowing soon, something was about to change in our lives. This would all pass and be behind us. It was June 12, 1976—her father's birthday, in fact. Arika appeared to have come around and was alert enough to share a vanilla ice cream with her daddy. Ice cream got all over her, sticky but good. Her dad had me pull the car over, and in a little spring of water, he washed his hands and Arika's sweet little hands and feet and face, like a baptism in a fresh spring! It appeared she was aware we were there and we were all together. Somehow that time shared in that ride took the fear and the emergency at hand out of our atmosphere. We drove on, surrounded by an unseen calming presence. However, all that changed as soon as we drove up to the canopy of the emergency room at Strong Memorial Hospital.

We had seen grace on our child as we traveled, but now that was gone. The staff that met us at the door were doctors and medical staff in emergency form, called off the golf course or the baseball field, called away from family or wherever their normal Saturday would have been spent—men and women swarming around this child, threatened by a mass on her spine. There were several; I didn't count. They all had a specialty, and they all seemed to know something we didn't yet know about the urgency of the reason we were finally at a medical center instead of at our local hospital, watching our daughter fade. Arika appeared to turn gray and pasty, the odor of sickness surrounding her as they took her from us. Was the grayness always there, the odor, the limpness, but kept from our senses as we traveled, to keep fear at bay? I don't know, but I did know I was relieved we were finally at a medical center; it gave me hope.

We didn't see our daughter for approximately the next five hours and, definitely, stacks and stacks of papers later. Finally, around 9:00 p.m. that Saturday evening, we were taken into a conference room, which held a long business table surrounded by office chairs. The room was stark but clean, sterile but did not smell as antiseptic as the halls we had been waiting in. We were introduced one by one to the team of medical staff by a lead physician who appeared to be in charge of the triage team.

He began, "I am Dr. Leo." He stated his headship and then, one by one, the staff too, stated their name and their position on the team.

With no medical background, the titles slipped through my mind. I was just grateful they were all there on Arika's behalf. It was true some of them had been called off the golf course due to the threat at hand.

Dr. Leo asked, "Do you know why you're here? Did anyone from the Corning Hospital inform you of the condition of your daughter?"

I spoke up and explained, "We were only told that she has a mass on her spine and that she needed to be transferred here. which I am grateful for, because I have been trying to get her transferred the past few days, but the hospital didn't appear to think it was necessary."

Dr. Leo seemed alarmed, "It is a good thing she was transferred without further delay." Then he proceeded to explain as much as possible in layman's terms what was happening to our baby girl.

Arika had a mass on her spine called a neuroblastoma. He explained it was a malignant cancer, which had started at the base of her spine, eroding the nerves that controlled her bowel and bladder, grew up the spine, traveled through the spinal column, wrapped around two ribs, and lodged on her lung—thus explaining the changes in behavior I had noticed with her bowel and bladder and the cause for the uncontrollable wetting, her feet seeming to hurt when she touched the floor, and progressing now causing the paralysis that prevented Arika from walking or sitting. He commended me for being a good historian, able to recall every detail of progressive change and when it appeared to happen. This cancerous tumor was aggressive. Dr. Leo told us this tumor could not be surgically removed. It was too vast and Arika's back too small. So he explained that she would be treated with radiation in increments of what he called "rads." I don't know anything about rads; however, I did know that he said what they were going to give her was massive amounts in order to attack the aggressive growth of the cancer cells.

They started that evening. Arika was marked with a blue permanent ink centering the tumor. She was placed in something that represented a cast to keep her head still. Her baby bottle was propped for her to be able to drink if she chose to. The machine seemed like exaggerated space equipment to me. I just watched speechless. Arika was placed in the terminally ill unit for children. She had a steel crib and was surrounded by children who, too, seemed lifeless—weakened by the attack of sickness with signs of hair loss or even more detrimental limb loss, darkened under their eyes, the joy of childhood gone, leaving blank stares and desperation in every glance. Some were not as bad as others, or seemed as threatened as some of the others. For those I was grateful; it meant some hope for them and us. They could get pulled in the unit's red wagon filled with stuffed animals and an IV pole following like a robot. I am not sure there are words that express what a child's terminally unit is really like. At our initial meeting with the medical team, Dr. Leo explained that Arika may or may not walk again—whether the paralysis was permanent was not yet clear. He talked about compression on the spine and erosion and words that ate at her cells. He did say, though, that she might not make it and that if she did, she may live a year—maybe two—no one could predict. But he made it *very* clear that this neuroblastoma, this cancer that had invaded our little girl's body, was life-threatening and that we could only know a day at a time what was truly ahead. Because Arika was in such a crucial state, the hospital placed a cot for me beside our daughter's crib in the terminally ill unit. I was not leaving her. I was not letting her leave me.

The first night at the medical center with Arika, I had no questions. I didn't ask God why or what was going to happen. I remember thinking and praying this:

"You know where we are, You know where Arika is, You made her. You know what is going on with her. All I know is that You are there and You said You would never leave me. You are here with us. That is enough."

And I recall being grateful that *finally, finally,* we had some answers as to "what" was happening to her. Knowing was better than watching her fade and not knowing why or what was happening. The questions changed for me, though, the second night in the medical center.

CHAPTER 14

THE UNIT WAS STEADY. NURSES were seriously attentive to last-minute shift duties, preparing for the next shift to take the helm as they were drifting angelic-like in and out of the babies' rooms, watchful of settings on whirring machines and lights flashing over coded buttons and gauges to be read. For now, each child's life depended on their accuracy and their service. They appeared to know that well, in a no-nonsense movement about them. As the shift change went without any interruption of care to the terminally ill children in the unit and the night melted from light to darkness, I sat at the foot of my daughter's steel crib, studying her frail, exhausted little body. The hall lights around the circular central station outside each child's room had dimmed for the approaching evening's rest. Arika's father had left the medical center and headed back to our hometown; there were details and prayers to be requested. Pastor Ron and Sharon needed to be told and prayer offered.

I sat alone with Arika—watching, studying, witnessing the death that was present and threatening her life. I missed her. I missed her movements. I missed her baby sounds. I missed the look in her eyes that told me she would be okay. I missed holding her. I missed my baby girl. She lay still. She was motionless, ashen, appearing unconscious to any life around her.

"Oh my God, no, oh my God, no," my heart longed for her. "Don't leave me, Arika, don't go, please don't go."

In my next desperate breath, I did ask her God and mine a question. I prayed, "Father, if I ever heard Your voice, if I ever heard

You speak to me, please speak to me now. Do You want to take her home to You, or do You want me to believe for her to be healed and stay here with me?"

I yielded myself to His will, as painful as that was to yield. I knew no matter what was ahead, I could trust Him. Instantly, as if a branding iron seared in my heart's identity, He spoke. I heard no voice. I saw written, like a branding iron impression within me: 1 Peter 5:7.

I wasn't familiar with what it said, so I opened my book, my Bible, and read these words.

> Casting all your care upon Him; for He careth for you. Be sober, be vigilant; because your adversary the devil, as a roaring lion, walketh about seeking whom he may devour: Whom resist steadfast in the faith, knowing that the same afflictions are accomplished in your brethren that are in the world. But the God of all grace, who hath called us unto His eternal glory by Christ Jesus, after that you have suffered awhile, make you perfect, stablish, strengthen, settle you. To Him be glory and dominion for ever and ever. Amen.

I knew God had given me these words, His Words. And from these words, I would have faith. She would live. I knew the living Word of God had spoken. I knew I was to fight a fight of faith for my child's life. I knew the devil tried to destroy her and that her God, my God, was not going to let that happen. She would live. I had to resist death and stay steadfast in faith, believing the Lord's dominion on this earth for my child. I had to believe that God gave us Jesus! And the blood of Jesus made her healing possible.

That Jesus was Who He said He was and that He did what He said He did for us—they aren't just history words written in a book. They are His living Word written to us who believe that Jesus came to earth because God so loved us and made a way of truth and life for us. Every word Jesus spoke, every work Jesus did was true—straight from Father God! Jesus said, "I am the way, the truth, the life. No man comes to the Father but by Me." He is the only holy blood; all others are mere men. Jesus is Lord! Emmanuel! God among us! I wasn't letting go of any of this truth that the Holy Spirit had taught me from His Word. I held on everything He said and believed it. My daughter was going to live and move and walk and grow and be healthy. I put my head on these promises written in the Bible and went to sleep by my paralyzed child that night, knowing I had been given faith for my child to live.

I kept that faith; even in the morning when the smell of cancer was still threatening—when her little body was still lifeless and her radiation treatments kept her too long from me and I couldn't hold her—I kept the faith. I kept the faith when negative reports came, saying they had to give her excessive rads. I kept the faith when I could still see the pale color of her being and the limpness of her body. I kept the faith when I saw no changes. I kept the faith—the faith of the Lord; I believed Him. I didn't believe what I saw or what I smelled or what I heard. I believed His Word to me. I kept His faith in me. I kept the faith that Jesus is Who He said He is—God in the flesh, the fullness of the Godhead bodily—and that He did what He said He did in the scriptures. I wasn't giving that truth up for anything. The Lord showed Himself faithful to me by reminding me of His words that said, "Your faith should not stand in the wisdom of men, but in the power of God" (1 Corinthians 2:5, KJV). "I am determined to know nothing among you, except Jesus Christ and Him crucified" (1 Corinthians 2:2, KJV). These words, "Fight the good fight of faith!" ran through my being like the air I breathed. "Fight … the good fight … of faith … Fight the good fight … of faith" (1 Timothy 6:12, KJV). Over and over, these words became a part of my being. I was going to fight this demonic cancer in Jesus's name on behalf of my child who could not fight for herself.

He reminded me of the woman who touched the hem of Jesus's garment and was healed. A throng of people were pressing up against Jesus during that healing. He turned to the one to whom He felt the healing virtue flow from Him. Why? Because she was the one who believed Him. She thought to herself, if she could only touch the hem of His garment, she would be healed, and she was healed when she touched His hem. Immediately, Jesus knew and asked who touched him. Many people had touched Him; many were touching Him at that time. But He knew someone touched Him, believing Him, believing Who He was and what He said. She was afraid, but Jesus told her, "Daughter, thy faith hath made thee whole" (Mark 5:34, KJV). "You are blessed because you believed that the Lord would do what He said" (Luke 1:45, KJV).

Is it easy? No, it isn't! Is it magic, where you can just throw out the name of Jesus and get what you want? No, it isn't! It's a relationship of love and trust and living in the Spirit. Jesus is no respecter of persons. He doesn't care what social class you're crying out to Him from. I was nobody. I was a young woman who had made many mistakes in life and who would make many more. And believe me, this healing was a fight. Even after receiving that scripture, I had a fight before me. One of the darkest days of my life came when the final radiation was over and they took an X-ray to show the results. I expected the tumor to be gone. I thought since I was given a WORD that this would be it, no more cancer—a clear reading and the doctor would tell me the good report. Didn't happen! The report was a bad one: the tumor was present still, shrunk a bit from the rads, but still threatening and still present! I stood outside the phone booth, waiting for the caller in it to finish their call so I could call someone—someone who would hear my heart's cry, someone who had faith, someone who could explain to me how you can believe and still not see the results. What happened? I knew I heard from God. I knew I believed Him.

Why was the cancer still present? Why was the X-ray showing a threatening neuroblastoma in her spine?

"Sister Glory, is this you?" I cried.

"Yes, Kelly, what's wrong [people called me by my maiden name for years], are you okay?" She must have heard the fear and desperation in my voice.

"No, no, I'm not. I'm scared, I'm confused, and I'm afraid," I couldn't stop crying.

She calmed me down as I began to explain the cause of my emotions and that recent X-ray and how the second night in the medical center, I heard from God and I knew I heard from God, but why then was the X-ray showing a tumor?

I clamored on, "Why would a cancer still be there if I knew God had healed her?"

I was new in the things of the Lord in the way of the spirit realm. I had only been saved two years. Sister Glory was not. She walked with God faithfully for years and was a woman minister I trusted, who worshipped at our church in Hornell. I knew I could trust her counsel.

"Kelly, don't doubt God's Word or His ways. Keep the Word He has given you. How He heals is not yours to say, just trust what you know He has said to you."

She continued to say these kinds of statements to me. I found my fear diminishing and my trust coming back. Faith had overcome fear. I had determined right then that the fear of the disease was as bad as the disease. I would stay on guard that fear did not steal my faith in the Lord. Faith works by love. I was going to stay in the love of the Lord, believing He does all things well and He has us in the palm of His hands. It was enough. I hung up the phone less confused, more aware, and very, very, grateful for people like Sister Hodge, people of faith. The following days, I stayed focused on the Lord and His teachings. I listened to a CD set by Kenneth Hagin. His voice echoed what the Lord had impressed within my heart and mind.

"Fight the good fight of faith … Fight the good fight of faith." Being vigilant was important to me now. I would be diligent, sober, vigilant, constant in season and out. It was no time for me to be weak or afraid.

I learned many lessons of faith during this time in Arika's life. That dark-day hurdle was one of them.

Another lesson came one day when I was in the waiting room of the terminally ill children's unit. A stranger started a conversation with me as I sat in the quiet of the waiting room, reading. Arika was taken for medical purposes. I spent the times that she was taken away from me by reading. This stranger sauntered in to the waiting room and sat down near me, engaging me into conversation. At first it appeared very innocent to me—although for some reason, which I was not yet aware of, this woman creeped me out! She asked me questions about my daughter and what was happening in her life. At first I thought her intention was just friendly, caring compassion. However, the conversation soon turned to her words of total chaos to me. Finding out my daughter was going to be a year old in a matter of days, she proceeded to interpret what this must mean astrologically!

Arika was a Cancer, and she started professing, "She is a Cancer, and that is why she is dying of cancer!" Her manner was intrusive, rude, and out of the norm of social interaction with a stranger! I immediately recognized the spirit in this woman, who pronounced death over my daughter!

I stood up very authoritatively and said, "Don't you dare speak those words over my daughter! She is not going to die, and I will not have you declaring these words over her life!"

I immediately exited that room and did not care a bit what the woman thought of my reaction to her and her horoscope! She was speaking death, and I rejected every syllable of it! I fully believe our words carry creative power. I learned a lesson of vigilance and confession of truth. Not long after this incident, the hospital staff came to me to tell me that a social worker would be coming to see me to talk with me. They thought that I needed to get away from the hospital for a while and spend a night or two in a local home available for the parents of children who were terminally ill. I met the social worker and listened to her words, though I must truthfully say, none of them were words of faith.

Yes, she was kind. Yes, she was considerate of Arika's circumstances and ours. Yes, she was sweet and very polite. But definitely, it was obvious to me that she did not believe my daughter would live, and it was her job to help comfort the reality of it, cushion the loss, and prepare me for Arika's death. The social worker wanted me to "walk with her from the hospital to the home of these kind people who would lodge me for a few nights of relief from the medical center atmosphere and the stress of the reality that Arika was not doing well." I decided, since Arika wasn't in her room (they took her daily for treatments and tests) and since I had the time, I would walk and check out the place they wanted me to stay for a few nights—except as soon as I left the hospital and started walking on grounds outside of the hospital property, I felt an immediate unction to not go!

I stopped abruptly and said, "No, I'm not going. I'm not leaving Arika! I want to go back to the hospital right now!"

The social worker, in her kind manner, tried to get me to change my mind.

"No, I'm not going anywhere. I'm not leaving her. I'm not sleeping anywhere except right by her! Thank you, I appreciate your concern, but I am definitely not leaving Arika."

Reluctantly, she allowed me to return to Arika's room. The social worker never interacted with me again. Another lesson, people may find me odd for my beliefs. However, the need to be near Arika and stay strong for her seemed important to me. Somehow, to me, if I left her, it would make her more vulnerable to death, and I wasn't going to have it. I wasn't giving in to any notion that supported loss of Arika, no matter how well intentioned or innocent. It just wasn't going to happen. I was staying as close to her every possible chance I had. I was aligning myself in faith agreement with the Holy Spirit, in word and action. I needed to remain close to Arika to do that.

At the conclusion of Arika's radiation treatment, Dr. Leo held another team meeting with the medical staff—including my husband and me—to discuss where they were in Arika's plan of treatment. At this meeting, an X-ray was shown to Gene and me that clearly showed the neuroblastoma had, indeed, shrunk but was still present. I was not shaken this time by the X-ray. However, the doctor informed me that they would start chemotherapy now on Arika, as there was no more radiation they dared give to her. They were already over the normal amount of rads they would want her to have. I didn't know how I felt about this chemotherapy. Dr. Leo had explained the process. Blood would be drawn from Arika and mixed with these chemicals, then that mixture would be transfused back into her system. It would be given to her through the top veins of her little hand. It could cause some burning. I wanted to wait.

"Could I have time to pray about this?"

It was at this question that I found out, I had already signed the release for Arika to receive chemotherapy. It was one of the many, many papers I signed the late afternoon of the day we brought our daughter to the medical center.

"Okay, then I guess you may go ahead with the chemotherapy treatment."

The doctor explained that the chemicals being used (they had names I cannot remember or would not know how to spell) would attack the cancer cells that multiply rapidly, destroying these cells. However, he warned that this also means that other cells are also attacked. I thought of brain cells, blood cells, bone cells, hair cells; it didn't seem to settle in my spirit. How could healing take place when something was working against her wholeness? To me, this felt as if it would undermine her healing, not help it. Dr. Leo also informed Arika's father and me that they would like to include Arika in a research study that was being done through a medical center in Ohio. He reported that this type of cancer—a neuroblastoma—was very rare in a child Arika's age.

"No, I don't want her to be in a study or in any trial for testing chemicals. I really don't even want her to receive chemotherapy, but I have signed the paper, so I will go forward."

I left that meeting with no peace but very troubled. I had no peace at all. Her father left and went back home. The chemotherapy would start.

I was very troubled in my spirit. Something was not right. I had no peace. The day after Arika's chemotherapy began, I was in the chapel of the medical center—praying, praising God and seeking Him. I liked the quiet sanctuary of the chapel. I was encouraged by the words I read on the wall: "Peace I leave with you. My peace I give unto you. Not as the world giveth, give I unto you." I knew that was from the Bible, John 14:27. That verse goes on to say, "Let not your heart be troubled, neither let it be afraid." This is exactly what I needed to "see." In seeking God, whether Arika should receive this harsh chemical into her body, I felt an emphatic *no*. That was all—no lightning bolt, no spoken word impressed—just a strong *no* in my spirit. I then started to express myself to my Lord. He heard me cry that I was tired.

I said, "Lord, I'm so tired. It isn't that I don't believe you. I do believe you, but I'm tired. I don't want to quit or give up faith, but I need a rest, just like if I was running and sat alongside the road for a rest, still headed in the direction I'm running, but with a rest alongside of the road. Would it be okay to rest, Lord? I need to weigh this *no* in my spirit. I need to get grounded again and know your will. May I rest, Lord, and lay this all down for now?"

I worshipped Him after this prayer and took the elevator back up to the floor that held my child and the other terminally ill children.

As I stepped from the elevator, Dr. Leo greeted me. It appeared as if he had been looking for me. He seemed excited to see me! I wasn't sure what the root of this enthusiasm meant, but as puzzling as it was to me, I was glad to see him! He told me he wanted to talk with me and directed us into Arika's room. He very compassionately started to tell me in these words.

"Mrs. Cook, we want you to have a rest. We have discussed the hesitancy you have in allowing your daughter to receive chemotherapy, and our team felt it would be good for you to take Arika home for a week and have a rest."

Wait a minute! Only God knew I had just prayed this to Him! Only God heard my heart that I wanted—no, *needed*—a rest!

The doctor continued, "We believe after you have your daughter home for a week, you will see the need for this treatment and understand the crucial state your child is in, allowing the treatment without doubt or fear."

I, in tears, expressed, "Thanks. When can we go?"

He explained some paper processing and some formalities, even explaining that this would not interrupt anything in her treatment, as there was a "schedule" for the chemicals and in between time of the doses.

"Fine with me. This couldn't be more timely, thank you."

I truly loved and appreciated Arika's treatment team. They were a medical staff who gave their service and gifts day in and day out, seeing some of the saddest situations in life yet continuing in giving their all. I called Gene; he came and picked us up. We were going home. Arika and I were going home and would return in a week to Strong Memorial. For now that's all I needed, to take my child home—out of this environment, out of the pain all around us—and sleep in our own covering, our own space. It felt as if we were going home to rest on our own holy ground.

CHAPTER 15

I WANT TO GO ON record saying, I am *not* telling anyone to take their child, self, or their loved one off chemotherapy—or any other medication, for that matter. What you do, or don't do, is between you, your loved one, and God. When there were healings in the Bible, Jesus made it clear that He is the Lord that heals us, but the how-to is between you and Him. Sometimes He spit and made clay, rubbing it on the eyes of the blind. Sometimes He instructed to wash in the river seven times. Sometimes He just said, go, or rise up, or lose Him. Whatever way He chooses is between you and Him. So before you read on, understand that I'm not telling you what your experience ought to be. I'm only telling you what mine was. I hope it encourages your faith. I hope it touches your life in any small way. I hope, above all, that it shows you Jesus to the glory of God our Father!

I returned home with my daughter. I soon realized I could not talk with others. I was getting too much sympathy and judgment too, and not enough faith from those around me. I decided after the first day and others stopping by to see us out of their sincere kindness and concern, that I didn't want to see anyone—even though they meant no harm. Their sympathy and fear after seeing Arika under-mined my faith. I didn't want to see people from the church. I didn't want to hear the "But what if," or "Well, you know, the Lord giveth and the Lord taketh away." I didn't want to hear that it was pride that I was being bold or expecting healing. I made a decision that I would see no one. I would talk to no one, except for her father. I did allow my Bible teacher to visit, and she was so in tune with the Holy Spirit that she didn't even want to come into the house.

Cora stood on my doorstep and spoke to me, "I have only one thing to say to you after praying. You have the mind of Christ."

I thanked her, and she left.

After her visit, I saw no one again until I returned to the hospital with Arika. During that time home, I did rest, and I sought God privately. I stayed in my room with Arika by me. I read Matthew, Mark, Luke, and John—the first four books of the New Testament. I read everything Jesus said in those books. I believed everything He said. I read every healing He recorded in those books. I believed every healing I read.

During this visit home, I learned several lessons. Reading the Word only deepened and strengthened my faith in Jesus. I had no doubt that He was Who He said He was—God in the flesh, Emmanuel, for us, on our behalf. I had no doubt the shed blood and the sacrifice He made on the cross for our sin, our healing, our deliverance, and our reconciliation to God was exactly as He said it was. I realized, fear was the enemy we fight. I realized, anything fear-based would never come to pass. I even asked God once during this time, "Why did Mr. So-and-So die of cancer? He was a godly man who loved you," or "Why did Mrs. So-and-So, who sang in the choir and loved you too, die of cancer?" or this one or that one. I went on and on, bringing up every incident where I witnessed failure or death, to reason with the Lord.

He just spoke into my spirit and said, "Don't let what I can do for your daughter be taken from you."

I determined I would keep my eyes on Jesus and no one else! I would experience Jesus myself. I loved Him, and He was very personal to me. Once, when I was deep in prayer for Arika in my room, I had a vision. I saw a footprint of a child whose age appeared to be around the age of seven or eight, according to the size of the print. It was in a muddy area along a pond, and that imprint of that picture stayed in my mind. It wasn't a baby's footprint; it was as an older child's print.

I asked myself, "Could this mean God was letting me see something in the future?" He could see what I couldn't, but the Holy Spirit in me was eternal. "Was the Holy Spirit confirming something that was not yet seen in the physical realm by showing me something in the spirit?"

I remembered the scripture that says, "He calls those things which be not, as though they were" (Romans 4:17 KJV).

I kept that impression of the child's footprint in my heart. I stayed constant in His presence and stayed close to my daughter. The week home was only adding to my belief in Jesus and His Word. Arika appeared to rest too. It was a blessing not to have her taken, poked, prodded, distant. She stayed present with me. We had a special time bonding during our private week home. When it was time to return to the hospital, I was more convinced than ever that she would not be taking chemicals into her bloodstream. Of course, this news was very alarming to Dr. Leo and the medical team of physicians—including the oncologist, urologist, radiologist, and other department heads.

Arika was admitted back into Strong Memorial. A meeting was scheduled with Gene and me and the medical team not long after Arika's return. I was given a gift of faith, and it had settled for me that Arika was not to receive chemotherapy. I was given peace about no chemotherapy, and I was letting the peace of God rule my heart and step on Arika's behalf. I knew this would not be easy to tell Dr. Leo and the medical team. I knew that in the natural, my choice made no sense to them. I understood that. But my faith was going to stand in the power of God and not in the wisdom of man.

The day of the meeting came. Her father and I had already made our decision; there would be no chemotherapy treatment. The table was filled with more medical team than I remembered. There appeared to be a buzz in the atmosphere. I knew I was on the hot plate as I faced this team. Dr. Leo was wonderful, though. He started the meeting with very kind words and a natural compassion that let my heart at ease. He was such a good man and such a special person to me. After all, until that team told me what was going on with Arika and why she had become paralyzed, I had no idea what was even wrong! I had only watched her grow weaker up until this beautiful group of committed medical staff defined what I was up against. How could I do anything but love them for their work and their service? I did love them. And it wasn't easy to tell them that I was taking her home and that there would be no chemotherapy. But in my heart, I heard, "Tell them for me." And so I did. I told them that I appreciated them and sincerely loved them for all I had seen in them but that Arika was not going to be receiving chemotherapy and that I wanted to take her home.

You could have heard a feather hit the floor. The room went silent, and then small gasps and angst filled the room. Some of the gasps were expressions of fear or perplexity at the decision made; other gasps were disgust and a look of confirmation that I must truly be in shock. One at a time, rebuttal was expressed. Then Gene let me talk, and so did the medical team let me talk.

"I'm taking her home. I believe she is healed, that Jesus healed her when He died on the cross and shed His blood for our sins and for our healings, rising from the dead on our behalf. He alone holds the keys to life and death." I told them, "I believe He has healed her. I just can't see it yet. I believe it was done when I asked, but it just hasn't manifest physically yet."

I explained my belief about physical and spiritual realms and angels that are sent to the heirs of salvation. Then I shared about Daniel's prayer and how he prayed but the devil blocked the answer for twenty-one days, and how the angel told Daniel that from the first day that Daniel set his heart to understand and to chasten himself before God, that Daniel's words were heard and the answer was sent. I told them that I believe the devil was trying to block her healing.

I told them, "Jesus is Who He said He is and that He did what He said He did." I told them about how He healed in scriptures and how He is the same—yesterday, today, and forever—and how He loves us and how He never leaves us or forsakes us and is a very present help in times like this. I went on and on, confessing Jesus and my faith in Him and what He has done for us. I told them that faith is the substance of things not seen.

"She is healed, and it's finished. I cannot allow my daughter to have chemotherapy. I have no peace about giving this chemical to her and injecting this chemical mixed with her blood into her body. I feel that it will work against the healing that is hers in Jesus, and I just cannot see the reasoning in the natural for killing cells that are not cancer cells."

The room went silent for a brief moment after I poured out my heart and my beliefs and my reasons for not allowing Arika chemotherapy. There were all kinds of reactions, which I knew would probably be the case, but it did not weaken my faith.

One specialist spoke up and said, "We have seen children come in here who are as near-death as your daughter, whose parents have invested in fad diets and Mexico trips, claiming healing and statues and lighted candles, and you name it, and we've heard it. But those families brought their child back after they found out those gimmicks don't work, and then it's too late for us. If we could have saved them, it's too late now, they lost too much being taken away." He continued, "And that's what we're afraid of, any progress that Arika has made, you will be taking away from her."

I responded, "I understand what you are saying, but the difference is, I'm not taking her to any statues or to any healing places. I'm taking her to Jesus. He is the Healer."

The physician quickly responded, "You're going out on a limb."

"Yes, yes, I am, and my daughter is going with me."

At this point, Dr. Leo placed all of Arika's medical records—including her X-rays, which clearly exposed a cancerous tumor—on the table.

He pointed to them and said to me, "Look, look at this, can't you see the urgency here for your daughter? Can't you see this tumor that's taking her life? Do you not understand the severity of this?"

I looked as he pointed and tapped his hand on the pictures. There it was—that ugly tumor, that ugly cancer that stole from Arika, that neuroblastoma that tried to steal her from me.

I started to cry, "Yes, I understood. But I also know Jesus has healed her. He did it for her on the cross."

At this, another doctor spoke up and asked, "Who do you think you are that Jesus wants to heal your baby and yet there's a whole unit of terminally ill children in the same unit, losing limbs and hair and dying? Who do you think you are that your child is to be healed and they aren't?"

Immediately, God gave me grace. I answered, "Jesus did this for them too. But I don't hope that He did it for Arika. I know that He did."

With that said, Dr. Leo spoke up, "I'm going to let you take her home. I've never seen faith like this. But I want you to know she won't live six weeks without the chemotherapy treatment, and I just hope that you can forgive yourself when you realize that her death expedited because of your decision." He also added, "And at that time, the State will come in against you for not allowing treatment."

The room went quiet; not a breath was heard. I had nothing more to say except, "Thank you," which I said through tears as I prepared to leave the medical team and that long table where it all started weeks and weeks ago.

On my way out of the room, a Jewish physician walked up to me and said, "I want you to know that if your paralyzed child ever walks again, you've made a believer out of me." He hugged me and walked away.

Gene and I were left standing in the hall. We hugged and made preparations to bring our baby girl home.

Gene said, as I stood crying, "It's gonna be okay, Kel. You did the right thing." He just held me as I cried in this holy place with Jesus.

CHAPTER 16

IT WASN'T MANY DAYS AFTER that meeting that a friend of mine—the wife of the couple who had given me my first good leather Bible, "my book," the same Bible I've used since May of 1977—was with me. She was there for me as I was taking Arika home from the medical center. I counted her a very special friend and appreciated the support during this time in our lives. Arika slept all the way home and appeared to have a certain peaceful way about her. Maybe she knew the hard part was over. Maybe she sensed the battle was the Lord's and not ours. We were going home.

However, I would soon find out that there is a reality to the words, "Fight the good fight of faith." It wasn't immediate, but Arika started getting weaker again. She appeared to progressively grow worse. Though she didn't cry or seem to be in any pain, I could tell she didn't have the stamina she had prior to our being home. This time was not easy. I almost gave up three separate times, and if not for God's grace and mercy and His faithfulness, I would not have been able to do what I had to do.

The first time the devil challenged me and tried to make a liar out of Jesus, I felt fear. It happened because I could smell the deadly tumor odor coming from my child. I was afraid. Immediately, the Lord spoke to my spirit in a very personal way.

He said to me, "When you mail a letter to your mother, do you see it get delivered? Or do you have faith that she will get it?"

I answered, "I believe when I mail it, she will get it."

He said to me, "Believe me to deliver."

It calmed my anxiety, and my fears dissipated. As long as she wasn't in pain or crying or appearing uncomfortable, I was okay. Weeks passed; she maintained. The second time the devil lied to me and tried to make me lose my faith, I was thinking I was going to give up and take her back to Dr. Leo. It was Gene, her father, that kept me believing. Arika awoke and seemed unable to relax or rest or be comfortable, and I instinctively was going to respond to this by taking her back to Dr. Leo. I started packing a suitcase for the hospital, saying nothing. It was night, and I was just going to drive us back.

When Gene realized what I was doing, he asked me, "What are you doing?"

I told him, "I'm taking her back. I can't do this anymore. I'm going back."

Immediately, Gene responded loudly and physically, grabbing my shirt and speaking right into my soul, "No! No, you're not! No, kel, no! You're gonna keep doing whatever you've been doing! Those doctors can't fix her. She doesn't stand a chance there! You're gonna keep doing whatever you do. It's her only chance! Don't stop believing! You've made a difference. You can't quit now! Keep your faith in Jesus, Kel! You're not going back!"

His words ignited my faith. I wasn't going to quit believing Jesus, and I wasn't taking her back. Gene had a soul connection with me that made me realize that I was doing the right thing—reminding me, I had heard from the Lord that first night I asked Father God about whether He wanted to take her home or He wanted me to believe for her to be healed and stay here on earth. Gene snapped me back into truth. The devil was the liar. Yes, our marriage was tough and our relationship strained; but we had some connection that, in spite of our differences, I knew if Gene could see my faith in Jesus, then I must be okay and just keep going.

Arika calmed and went right back to sleep, showing that it was my fear that I was giving in to. She hadn't yet manifested in healing, but that night my faith was restored that she would.

The final and third time that the devil tried to rob Arika of her healing, Gene and I were in bed. Arika was lying between us. It was the middle of the night and weeks after that last attack. Arika had not improved. She showed no sign of healing. The smell of the tumor was always present, but typically, she was calm and did not seem to be uncomfortable. However, this night I woke up to the most horrifying scream a child could make. It was bloodcurdling. Without an instant of delay, something rose up in me! The Spirit of Christ, the Holy Spirit, took over my being. I heard the scripture in my spirit, "Lay hands on the sick, and they SHALL recover!" I placed my hands on Arika's back and started to declare the Word of God over her. Immediately, the Lord put me in the spirit, and I could "see" into my child's back.

I lifted my hands from her and pointed to that tumor and commanded, "IN THE NAME OF JESUS, SATAN, LEAVE HER BACK NOW!" I started declaring loudly, "SHE IS A CHILD OF THE KING! SHE IS A CHILD OF LIGHT! SHE IS A DAUGHTER OF THE MOST HIGH GOD! SHE IS FROM THE KINGDOM OF LIGHT, AND THERE IS NO DARKNESS IN HER!"

I was shouting to the top of my lungs the words the Lord was speaking through me with declaration, authoritatively in the spirit. I don't even recall all that I did declare over her, as it was the Lord that gave me the words and they were not my own. As I declared the truth over Arika—of who she is and Who Jesus is to her—commanding that satan leave her alone in the name of Jesus, that tumor lifted from Arika's back—flying out of there! It hit my thumb and ricocheted into the air!

Arika instantly lay still, and for the first time in months since that June night when the Lord spoke to me that I would not be going into work, she lay resting like a toddler should. The smell of the tumor was gone. The atmosphere was different. There was calm and a presence that I had never known before. A sweet-smelling savor filled the air. It was over. The battle was over. She was healed. I took her back to the medical center the next day. Their report confirmed that Arika was definitely tumor-free.

The doctor noted, "The report showed that even scar tissue had been touched"—which, from what I gathered from the doctor, was shocking. It seems scar tissue is a different type of tissue that stays scarred—at least, that is how I interpreted what he was saying.

Tears were exchanged; blessings were exchanged; and praise was given to the Lord. But the doctor insisted, though, that I bring her for regular checkups—which I did for about six months, until they finally said that there is no need to keep bringing her back. She showed no more signs of cancer. They released her. She was no longer paralyzed or tormented by that neuroblastoma. Arika was healed. In Jesus's name, Arika was healed.

I would be leaving out some glory to God if I didn't share these updates. When Arika was about two years old and talking, one day when I was sitting on my bed—worshipping the Lord, legs crossed and my Bible open in front of me—Arika was playing near me in the room.

She, out of the blue, said, "I saw you with your book, Mommy, when Jesus took me with Him and 'Hims' made my black bones white bones!"

I was shocked! "What? What do you mean, Arika?"

She proceeded to tell me that she saw me sitting with my book and Jesus took her and that He said, "Don't be afraid, Arika. I'm going to send you back to Mommy." She said, He told her, "I'm sending you back, and all I want you to do is love Me."

Then she started sharing how there is a big picnic and we're all gonna go! And she said she had three brothers there. (Arika at that time was an only child.) I don't care what your theology is; today Arika has three brothers, no sisters! There's no way she could have known that except through Christ.

When Arika was about seven years old, I was with her outside by our pond. I was watching her play and enjoying the wind and the sunny day. She was building a mud castle at the pond's edge. We were talking back and forth and laughing and being silly, when I noticed the picture of the footprint I had seen during the week that I took her out of the hospital and had taken her home to pray—the week I was trying to decide whether she should receive chemotherapy. There it was…the child's impressed footprint—not of a baby, but of a little girl. There it was—the vision he had given me of a healed child's footprint! It was my daughter's footprint—not a paralyzed child, but a walking, talking, laughing child.

Finally, another glory to God!

When Arika was sixteen, we lived in Massachusetts. I took her to the Dana Farber Cancer Institute for a checkup. I reported the history about the neuroblastoma that had attacked her and she had been healed from.

When I told the doctor that I had not allowed her to receive the treatment of the chemotherapy, he looked at me stunned and then, to my amazement, said, "That's the best thing you could have done for her. They have discovered that the treatment of that chemotherapy crystalizes in their heart." He told me, "That was wisdom."

I assured him it wasn't my wisdom! I reminded myself right then of the words that God taught me: "to let my faith stand in the power of God and not in the wisdom of man." I was grateful that the Lord knew what I could not have known when I wouldn't allow the chemotherapy treatment. I since met a mother whose child recently died from that crystallization in her heart. It grieves me for her loss. It reminded me of that season in my life where cancer tried to devour us.

When I was at college, getting my bachelor's degree, I met a pastor that I thought might be interested in the recorded testimony I have of Arika's healing. I gave him the recording, and he took it home, returning it a few days later. When he gave it back to me, something felt uneasy to me. I looked at him and expected a response of how good God is or how His Word is true or how His mercy endures forever or how we overcome by the blood of the Lamb and the Word of our testimony. I mean, he's a pastor, right? So the people of God are fed by God's shepherds, His pastors, right? I expected the Lord to be praised and hope given.

Instead, he looked at me, handing me the CD, and said, "You don't believe that healing is for everybody, do you?"

I was shocked and felt sad for the people of God. Just so you know, according to the Word of God, Jesus came to forgive our sins and to heal us, and He is no respecter of persons. Will everyone get saved? Will everyone get healed? I believe we have a part in bringing truth to pass. Once, I was asked by a pastor not to share my testimony in the church.

"Some people may be offended."

My heart breaks over these kind of responses from pastors. It's sad to me when a pastor hands back my testimony and says, "Interesting," and won't open their pulpit to have faith shared.

I pray that what you have read of Arika's healing builds your faith in Jesus and that you realize He is no respecter of persons and that He is the same yesterday and forever. I am nobody special. In fact, as you continue to read my story, you'll see I messed up many times after this. I'm not perfect. I have no works that saved me. But I know what it is to love Jesus and to be loved by Him. No one can take that from me. If you don't hear this message from a pulpit, I hope you heard it in my book: Jesus died and rose again for your sins and for your healing.

Today Arika is forty-one years old—a beautiful, healthy woman of God. She and Tim have blessed me with three grandchildren— Nickolas, Luke, and Ava Rose. And I realize, as I tell her story and mine, that I'm telling you this—as Arika said—"for Hims."

"He made my black bones white bones."

Jesus is the author and finisher of our faith. The words *Tell Them for Me* resound in my soul, and now that I've told you, please go tell someone for "Him."

CHAPTER 17

I HAD A DREAM. I was driving down the road in my Volvo, and as I looked in my rearview mirror, a tractor trailer truck was so close to me I couldn't see its headlights—only the grill, which covered the vision of my back window. I realized, up ahead, there was a child—a toddler eighteen months to two years. She had walked out in the road, right in front of me. If I kept driving, I would hit her. If I put on my brakes, the truck would plow over us. But I felt no choice. I started braking. The truck somehow shifted down, braking, and didn't flatten me, and I was able to prevent the child from being hit. I jumped out of my car and picked up the little one. There were no cars around, no houses, and no people. Then off to the left in a field, I noticed a long, old black Cadillac. The door on the driver's side was open. From the distance, I could see a woman in the front seat. I walked over, carrying the child. When I reached the car, she jumped out hysterically and threw a huge knife at the baby. I reached out and caught it, stopping it from hitting the child's back. The knife turned to ashes in my hand. The baby wasn't harmed. This was only a dream, but I realized that my subconscious state described what I felt over the months I was believing for my child's life. The devil did try to destroy her and take her from me, but God turned the enemy's power to ashes.

I would like very much at this point of my story to tell you that after Arika's healing, everyone lived happily ever after—except I think the enemy hated me more than he ever had. It appeared that in this lifetime, I would never truly be wanted or know a faithful, true relationship from a man. If so, it would certainly take some time and some heartbreaks and rebellion. I did not want to be alone. Gene and I went through a divorce. It wasn't pretty. No divorce is; it's heart-wrenching. He had gone back into the world's ways, and I had lost my ability to love as I should. I couldn't forgive myself for not being able to have faith for us.

I was tired, and I quit trying. It wasn't that I didn't love him. I did. I just couldn't keep forgiving him, and then I couldn't forgive myself. I ended up seeking help in the church. That turned out to be a nightmare.

It was the '70s. No church had counsel that accepted divorce; it didn't matter what had happened in the marriage. Divorce was ungodly, and there was no help. I was judged and told by a pastor's wife that I wasn't fit for the kingdom. I really did try to stay in the church, but I was depleted enough that I turned away. I couldn't have faith for me to change. I wanted to be cared for and loved and respected and honored, and I wanted it to be Gene. But when none of those were realities in our marriage, I left. He was free to do and be whatever he wanted. I was done. But I left so broken that I turned to all the wrong answers. I got too close to a Christian brother and felt an emotional connection that scared me. I ran so that I wouldn't make him fall from grace too, and instead, I started a relationship with a man a friend at work that wasn't in our so-called Christian circle. I was feeling some safety and security in our friendship—at least, that's how it started out. He was a good man. Outwardly, you may have even thought he was a Christian. He didn't smoke or drink or do drugs or swear or any of those unreligious signs! His parents were born-again, and every sibling was too. We worked together and shared many long conversations. I went to lectures at the college with him. I rode horses with him. We communicated about authors, talking for hours. I started drinking coffee! We enjoyed gardening and built fences together. We went antiquing, and I learned the difference between an oak table and a pine one! We walked in the woods, and he could name every tree we passed. I found him interesting and engaging. It was a break from the intensity I was used to in my marriage. It was fun sharing life with someone.

At first our relationship was harmless. But when Gene realized I was seeing someone, even though he and I weren't together, his PTSD came out big time. I was afraid of him, and he gave me reason to be. The enemy used that fear to drive me closer to a man that started out as my friend. I ended up giving up my apartment and moved in a father-in-law apartment adjacent to this man's home. I was running away, and I knew it. I just didn't care anymore. I felt that I had given all I could.

Moving was just a way I excused my sin. Gradually, I didn't read my Bible anymore. I quit the church and stayed away from all my Christian friends. The enemy made them all seem different to me. I couldn't understand them or their ways or their audacity to be so judgmental toward one another. Soon I was in sin over my head. Oh, it all seemed very innocent at first, but it wasn't. I felt guilt and shame, and I missed being close to God. I didn't realize that once called by Jesus, He never really leaves you. He is a jealous God and won't let anything separate you from Him! Thank God for that grace and mercy! Because I looked for love in the wrong place, it almost cost me my life and my soul.

While living in that sin state, my companion had given me a horse as a Christmas present. I was out in the pasture with Mykel—my new, beautiful spotted Appaloosa—and I, being a novice to riding, had given Mykel too much lunge line. She bolted forward, taking the line and kicking her hind legs into the air. Her two back legs hit me square in my chest and flipped me backward, knocking me out. I started passing through this tunnel speedily. On the sides of the tunnel were people speaking, but I couldn't understand a word they said.

My thoughts at that instant were, *Where am I? If I don't know where I am, where is Arika? Who is taking care of Arika?* I wished someone was speaking English so that I knew where I was or where I was going.

Suddenly, I heard, "Kelly, Kelly!"

I immediately turned, recognizing that was a name I knew, and I followed it back through the tunnel. I was back in my body. My friend was slapping my face, shouting, "Kelly, Kelly!" at me. I was taken to the hospital emergency room. Mykel kicked my ribs into my chest, bruising my heart. I could have died, except for God's mercy. I was living in sin. I knew I would have gone to hell if I had died. Even though I was not serving the Lord, I knew His Word was *yea* and *amen*, and unrepented sin has its price.

As soon as I recovered from that accident, I moved into a ministry house with five other Christian women. I rented a portion of the house that gave Arika and me our own little apartment. I tried—and I say *tried*—to serve the Lord. But it was hard! Nothing felt the same. I missed my friends, and so did Arika. His family was good to us. It was a hard time for me. Emotionally, I was drained, thinking of getting married. Arika would wait and wait for Gene to come and pick her up at times when he said he would get her and then he wouldn't show. Due to our situation, the courts ordered that Gene had to pick Arika up in a public place, so she and I would sit in McDonalds and wait and wait. When he didn't show and I tried to leave, she wouldn't want me to, saying he would come and we would miss him. When he would come, his new wife would be with him and say things in a singsong mocking voice, like, "Having a good day, Kelly?" knowing that Arika and I had waited and waited and waited for him.

It was too painful, all of it. I wanted a nest, a home, a safe place to fall for Arika and me. Had I been smart, I would have fallen into the arms of Jesus. Instead, I rebelliously and foolishly chose the arms of flesh. I lusted after the flesh, and believe me, it had a high cost. I think, during some of those times, Gene would have gone back with me. I did miss him, but I wasn't going to give in to my emotions about him. Lionel Richie's songs always made me miss him and James Taylor and any music that had been part of our magic-carpet rides. But I was not living like we had anymore; besides, he was married now. I could forget him. I married my friend to excuse myself from sin—at least, that's what it feels like, now. I am sure that is not what I thought at the time. Then I thought it the most intelligent decision I had ever made! We had a Christian wedding officiated by the pastor of the church we attended together. We still had great coffee times and long conversations. His parents were delighted he had married a "Christian girl."

They were really wonderful people and favored Arika, making her life full of good experiences. She had her own pony at the farmhouse and climbed the trees in the chicken yard. She had a best friend she rode bikes with that lived in a farm down the road. We had a pond and lots of woods to roam and had lots of picnics in the woods. Yet soon into the marriage, I knew it was the biggest mistake I had ever made, because the nest I wanted and the more children I wanted all of a sudden weren't acceptable to him. He decided he wanted no more children. How could this be? We had discussed this in length prior to our marriage. I knew in my heart I had a son. But he wasn't going to allow me to have any more children, and that was that. He wanted a vasectomy. I wouldn't sign for it. (In our state, the spouse has to be in agreement; I wasn't).

It ended up that I had gotten so far from the truth of God that I had anxiety and was under great stress. It honestly felt as if a cosmic joke had been played on me—something so much bigger than I that I wasn't sure how to get back to where I was. I resigned myself to sign for him then soon fell into a depression.

It became so bad, and it took me months to get out of it. Slowly, he appeared to be charmed by my best friend, Sophia, and the dynamic between them was very clear to me. We lost the farmhouse and ended up living in a mobile home that I purchased from my working at the factory. We lived in it three months while he kept promising that the electric, sewer, and gas would be completed. It was totally opposite of all the promises made and the conversations had. However, I hung in there. I figured, I made my bed, I would lie in it.

The depression became more severe. Unless you have been through the darkness of depression, I really have no words for it. The darkness swallows you up. I couldn't talk to people anymore. If the phone rang, I was anxious; it was probably a bill collector. I couldn't go to the market without panicking in the parking lot; it all felt so overwhelming. The walls at work seemed to close in on me, until eventually I was placed on disability. I could not function. I was so far from God I did not know how to get back, how to get back, how to get back. I was depleted.

One day during the darkness I was living in, I closed myself in our bathroom where I would not be bothered if he came home. Arika was at school. I sat on the floor and cried and cried my head in my hands. I didn't know how to go on or get back to some light. It was like every force in hell was against me. When I would try to get back to Christ and the peace I knew from Him, it seemed impossible.

I cried out to God, begging, "Please, please, help me. I don't know how to live. I don't know how to be here. I feel like I'm so far from you, Lord, and I just don't know how to get back, to get out of this sadness and overwhelming feeling of loss. Please help me."

I sat for hours, shutting myself up in the privacy of that room. When it was close to the time Arika would be home from school, I desperately prayed, "Lord, I have to function. I have to quit crying. Arika cannot see me this way. I don't know how to go on. I don't know how to live. Help me."

Clearly, this is what I heard: "Get up. Turn the doorknob. Take one step into the hall, walk a step at a time. In Me you live and move and have your being."

I did exactly what the Lord told me to do. I met Arika without any tears or alarm to her. I was able to be at peace for her. Today, all these many years later, I absolutely know I can do nothing without Him. I can't even turn a doorknob without Him. I wouldn't want to. My battle wasn't quite over yet; the Lord was about to show Himself strong on my behalf. Little did I know, all this time that I fought that oppression and depression, it was the enemy trying to destroy me.

Father God was not going to let me self-destruct. Looking back on it, I opened the door to the enemy ignorantly in rebellion. I let the brokenness of my heart excuse my actions. I played into the devil's hands. But I learned that you don't take a single morsel from his table without destruction following that morsel. You may think, "Oh, it's just a bit of this or that," as you eat or drink at his table blindly. But when you get ready to leave that table, you will find he has hand-cuffed you to the tables leg; you aren't going anywhere. At least, that is what he would like you to think. But God … God is greater. His mercy endures forever.

As I said, my battle wasn't quite over yet. I still isolated myself from church and from my friends. I found it difficult to interact, which was not the norm at all for me. I had always been a lively, strong, friendly, socially adept woman. It wasn't the case now. I never felt good enough around other people, especially Christians. I felt like they were good and I wasn't. They were holy and godly and I wasn't. They knew how to walk this walk of being a Christian, and I didn't. I was plagued with self-doubt.

All the time, though, I never stopped seeking God in it—in whatever way I knew how to. Even when it didn't work and He seemed forever away, I didn't stop crying out to Him. I thanked Him for all He had done for me and all the times He was there for me. I couldn't feel a thing except inner pain, but I kept calling to Him.

Then one day, a Sunday morning, while I was lying in my bed—the covers up over my head, hiding myself—I heard Him again.

"Get up. Just as you are, get to the church." I had blue jeans and a baggy sweater on. I thought to myself, *Just as I am? I look terrible.*

He said, "Go. Go quickly."

So I did.

I went to the church. I sat in the last pew. I wanted to be left alone. I don't even know what pastor preached, but I know this. I heard him say two relevant life-changing things. First he said, "If you mean business with God, you will be here when those church doors are open." And the second thing I gleaned was a scripture. He said, "We overcome him by the blood of the Lamb, by the word of our testimony, and we love not our lives unto death" (Revelation, KJV). It was an aha moment for me. The devil was done keeping me isolated from worship and service. I would be there at that church whenever those church doors were open. And two, I would overcome by the blood of the Lamb. I would. I knew I would get back to who I am in Christ. It would take time, but I knew it would happen. I had finally seen a candle in the darkness. My hope was renewed.

Believe me, it didn't happen quickly; and it was something I had to walk out a step at a time, just like He said. I stayed in the Word, reading faithfully.

"Man does not live by bread alone but by every word that proceeds from the mouth of God" (Matthew, KJV).

I attended church regularly, even when I felt I was not getting one thing out of it. I kept going. I stayed public. I stayed with the body of Christ, even when I felt less than or unworthy. My fight might not be physical this time, but I would "fight the good fight of faith."

Then one weekend, the pastor was having a conference weekend at the church. There would be an all-night prayer meeting following the Friday night service and then meetings on Saturday night and Sunday morning. I was going to be at them all! My husband had stopped going to church soon after we were married—of course, he did!

He would drop me off at our church and then go get his Dunkin Donut coffee and *The New York Times* and wait for me outside in the parking lot. So I was aware he wouldn't be at all these meetings, but there would be no way I was going to miss them. I went Friday night, and little did I know at the time, that service was the beginning of new life for me. It started when I got to the church. I was still struggling with feeling depressed, but I kept doing what the Lord told me to—which was, be in the church when the doors were open, don't stay away, and we overcome by the blood of the Lamb. I knew it wouldn't be my power getting me out of the depth of the depression. I clung to those two realities. Walking into the first service that Friday night, I saw a big white limousine pull up to the front door of the church, and three adults got out of the car—two men and one woman. They were dressed to the hilt, not a hair out of place.

Immediately, I said to myself, "I hate her!" Then instantly, I thought, *What are you thinking, you don't even know her!* I felt shame for even having such a bad thought! I repented and said, "Lord, you know I don't hate her, I don't even know her!"

Something in me totally resisted her. We walked into the church around the same time. Come to find out, she was the guest minister speaking that night at our service! During the course of the service, there was an altar call for anyone needing prayer. I went forward, believing for my husband who was out of work that some work would come his way.

When I stood in front of her and told her why I was there and what my need was "work for my husband," she said—looking right into my soul—"Honey, yes, we'll pray about this work for your husband, but even greater than that, I want you to know that God has a deliverance for you."

That's all she said; she didn't pray anything special over me. She prayed about my husband's work and then just asked me if I would be back for service the next night, and I said, "Yes, I would." Something had happened to me, though, at that altar: my heart felt softened.

But I did not know what she meant when she said "God has a deliverance for you." What did she mean?

I stayed after the service for the all-night prayer. Only a handful of us were there. We prayed through the night, seeking the Lord on behalf of the conference that weekend. I asked some of the others that were there what she meant when she said that God had a deliverance for me. They just told me not to worry about it. I did worry about it. I wanted to know what she meant.

The morning came. I went home and rested, waking refreshed and getting my housework done before the night service. Returning to the church that night dressed in my black-and-white checkered sundress, I was anxious and excited about the service. Worship and praise began; the Word of God was ministered; and then she said, "Little one in the white-and-black checkered sundress, come up here."

It was obviously me. I walked to the front of the church. She then called for every pastor that was in the house to come forward, and because it was a conference, there were around seven or so of them. She stood in front of me with my hands in her hands. She looked into my eyes and started talking.

"You've had a very hard time, haven't you? You've tried to serve and do what is right, but you have been prevented from peace and rest, haven't you?" She continued speaking. I was nodding in affirmation, tears pouring down my face. "You made it through a very difficult battle, and the devil has tried to wipe you out ever since. He has lied to you, he deceived you. You've been battling depression and thoughts that are not yours, and a darkness so thick that you've even wondered how you could get back to that personal place in Jesus."

All the time, I was crying, relieved that someone actually knew what I had been going through. I had been fighting this for years on my own—years in deep sadness, years trying to be me.

"Dear one, you had a great victory, and since then, the devil has tried to shut you up, to isolate you, to prevent you from the joy of the Lord. He has even used your relationships against you." I could not stop the tears. "He tried to kill you, but God spared your life. He has stolen, but God will restore and give you the desire of your heart." I knew that was the son I wanted that I was being prevented from conceiving. "Well, honey, your battle is over! Tonight the Lord is going to deliver you! The devil is not going to oppress you anymore!"

She ordered the pastors to make a circle around me, and they started praying, "IN THE NAME OF JESUS, LEAVE HER ALONE, SATAN!"

They weren't holding back at all. Each one was declaring loudly over me, commanding the spirit to leave me alone in the name of Jesus! It was a battle that thing was resisting. At one point, I remember looking into my pastor's eyes, thinking, *I'm not going to leave her.*

No words—only thoughts—and my pastor said, "You don't have any choice! In the name of Jesus, you loosen this woman!"

I don't recall all the struggle; I clearly recall the deliverance. I was free. The torment was gone! I not only felt different; I saw differently—as if a fog or barrier had been taken from around me! A thickness had been removed!

The minister again put my hands in hers, and looking into my tear-filled eyes, she said, "Honey, you are an *eagle* in the kingdom!"

I was free! The fight was over! I truly was delivered! I went home free. I went home—me, who I am in Christ, without fighting every second for it. I realized where those thoughts came from when I had first seen that woman get out of that white limousine. They weren't mine; they were that of tormenting spirit, and it knew she carried the authority of the Lord Jesus Christ and knew its time was up! Hallelujah!

The next day, I was sitting by our pond, reading. As I sat there, all of a sudden, the ugliest, saddest-looking thing came before my face and started whining. It wanted me to feel sorry for it!

It whimpered, "I don't know what I'm gonna do. I don't know what I'm gonna do."

Jesus immediately spoke to my spirit and said, "Don't answer it, don't say a word, keep reading."

That thing departed as quickly as it manifested, and I have never fought depression again. I only have one lesson to tell you about this. One of the worst things you can ever do is feel sorry for yourself when you've been through loss or a broken heart, or been cheated or mistreated. It's a crack to let the devil torment and bring with him a tormenting spirit. Trust that all things work for your good. Don't give in to defeat or feel sorry about your situation or circumstances. The darkness wants you to agree with it. Don't.

It's okay to miss your children or loved ones; it's okay to long for love in your life; but recognize the difference between missing a loved one, wanting to be loved, and giving in to depression. I made the choice to forgive myself. I had more big choices to make. I had made mistakes. I wasn't a good, faithful partner. But I decided that escaping the truth of the way I felt wasn't going to make us a better couple. I left that unhealthy, unequally yoked bond I had made. I had to swallow my pride about what other people would think. To this very day, he lives with my once–best friend, Sophia.

They appear very happy together. He is still very good to Arika. His family was a safe place when she and I needed a safe place. I faced the judgment of walking away, but better to walk away than live a lie. Believe that the peace of God must rule your heart. If there is disruption, you need to search the truth of your own heart. I will tell you this: compromise will cause you to sin, and sin will lead you to destruction. You have to be true to yourself and God, no matter what the cost. Let God be the Judge.

CHAPTER 18

IN TIME, I TOOK AN educational leave from the Corning Glassworks where I was employed. They helped pay for my degree because I had ten-plus years with the factory. It was one of my benefits, besides the great insurance they carried that kept Arika and me covered! When she had cancer, it was that insurance that allowed us to pay for the extensive time of hospitalization. I attended Cape Cod Community College. I loved studying and learning and challenging myself. I went back to New York during the summers to work in the factory; that was a required part of the educational leave. I worked on the Cape too during my semester courses, doing internships in the social service field. The internships gave me credits and pay, which was very helpful for a single parent. I continued my leave during the college semester months. In a few years, I had completed my associate degree concentrating in the behavioral sciences. I loved Cape Cod so much I decided not to go back to CGW and continued living on the Cape, getting work in the human service field. I was free in Christ. I felt no regret about my decisions or my life. I attended a church and was satisfied with being alone. However, I had deep within me the longing for my son that I knew I had but could not yet see. It was as if I knew him and missed him. I would see babies with their mother, and something within me would ache for my child that I had not even yet seen! Again, God showed up on my behalf! I'm always amazed in our imperfections and even in our weakness of the flesh, how faithful He is! I never pretended to be perfect. I was too aware of the lust of my flesh and too conscious of not hiding myself from my flesh to pretend there was anything holy about me, except Him! It certainly wasn't my works that saved me! But the thing I did have in spite of my weak flesh was a sincere love for Jesus and a heart quick to repent when I missed the mark of my calling or if I knew I grieved Him. I couldn't stay off track long without the unction of the Holy Spirit convicting me of sin or compromise and helping me get back to the author and finisher of my faith. He repeatedly showed Himself faithful. He proved to me that nothing could separate me from His love.

I don't know if it was because I didn't have a solid childhood or parents that were there for me, but God sure was merciful to me in spite of my failures or weaknesses. He knew my heart concerning the son I carried within me. Scripture is clear. Read Psalm 139: He knew us before we were born. Something eternal within me knew I had a son. One day I went with friends to a tent meeting. An evangelist was preaching at the fairgrounds, and so this couple and I went together to hear the message of the gospel.

During the service, the evangelist offered that if anyone was carrying a burden that they needed to leave at the cross once and for all and not pick it up again, to come forward for prayer. He reminded us how we may have turned something over to the Lord but then may have taken it back again. This seemed to be the case for me concerning my son—a son I could not yet see. I thought of going forward about this when I heard the Lord's voice speak to me within, "I will restore the years the cankerworm hath taken."

Without delay then, I knew I should go forward. I didn't tell the evangelist what I was there for. I knew God knew. and I just let the evangelist pray for me to lay this burden down at the cross once and for all and not pick it back up. To my wonder, the evangelist stood over me and said, "The Lord would say to you, He will restore the years the cankerworm hath taken!"

Now, he had no idea that God had just spoken those very words to me, and here God was confirming to me that He heard my heart's cry! He confirmed the words He spoke to me through this evangelist! I returned to my seat, tears running down my face, my burden laid down once and for all.

Because of my tears, my nose was running and I asked the friend sitting next to me if she had a tissue. She said no; she didn't have one. Suddenly, behind me a tap on my shoulder, and a woman that I didn't know, a total stranger, said, "I don't have a tissue, but this is clean, and you may use it for your tears." She handed me a pure-white cotton-soft cloth baby diaper! I buried my face in that little diaper, and the sweet savor of an Almighty God comforted me.

Only my Father God would show such love, to me, a sinner saved by grace. No one knew what I had gone forward to pray about. No one knew it was the baby boy in my heart that I laid down at the cross. But my Father knew, and from that day forward, the ache in my heart for my son diminished. I knew God's timing would be perfect. Of course, it was.

Years later, I met John Joseph Costello III, who blessed me with John Joseph Costello IV. I'd like to say I met Jack when I was a lily-white Christian, behaving myself. It appears I wasn't. I had been told by the church I was attending that if I didn't return to my ex-husband, the judgment of God would be on me. It took me that meeting in the pastor's office and the few miles back to my house to decide I was done trying to please the church. I had even run into one of the members after that at the gym, working out, and she said to me, "If you want to do the will of God, you will get back into our church." That only made it more real to me that I would never go back there.

People running other people's lives in the name of the Lord! I just didn't get it. I could not understand and to this day do not understand what gives people who call themselves Christians the right to be telling other people what to do or judging them in the name of the Lord—like they have been given some freedom to judge and know God's will for someone else. You know God's will for you. People don't need to be telling you God's will for you! Father never accuses; He convicts and is long-suffering to lead us to repentance. He does not pounce on us like lions after a prey. Period. I have no tolerance for religion that judges self-righteously. Jesus had no tolerance for it either. I also have no tolerance for Christian groups that think they have the right to what they call prophesy (falsely) into lives of other brothers and sisters, speaking condemnation and sickness and judgment over them! It still goes on today!

Last Monday, I sat in a Christian group meeting to pray about our government and the upcoming election. Of course, a brother there decides to prophesy to me. Now, what was interesting was that the very first sentence he said, the Lord had spoken to me that morning. But he should have stopped after the first sentence because then he went on in the flesh, and I immediately stopped him.

"I'm not receiving those words. You aren't speaking that over me."

The room went silent, and then someone redirected to get back to prayer. I believe in the power of the creative word; what someone says over you carries power. Don't let people just say whatever comes to their mind over you. This takes great discernment because the Lord does use one another to exhort and speak encouragement to one another in order. However, remember when Jesus asked Peter, "Who do you say that I am?" And Peter answered, "Thou art the Christ."

Jesus let Peter know; flesh and blood didn't reveal this to him but our Father in Heaven. Yet only sentences later in the same chapter, Jesus is rebuking Peter and telling him, "Get thee behind me satan, thou art an offense unto me!" (Matthew chapter 17, KJV). So be aware, walk with discernment in the spirit, and be mindful of words spoken over you. The Lord will confirm by others something He has already told you, or something you already know. The Latin word *educo*—which is a base word for our English word *education*—means, "to draw out." God will draw out of you something that is within you.

This is a funny comparison, but did you ever hear that song by America with the lyrics, "Oz never did give nothing to the tin-man that he didn't already have?" You already have it! Be wise as a serpent, harmless as a dove (Matthew 10:16, KJV). Good will draw out of you the gift within you. Once, when I was having financial needs, someone started speaking over me that in five years, I would be financially well off. I stopped that man right there from saying such nonsense.

I said, "I don't receive that because I don't have to wait five years for my financial needs to be met. God will take care of me daily and meet my financial need daily."

It was this man's way of saying, "Hold on, you might be poor now, but God will bless you in five years!"

What? I felt like, "You're kidding me, right?" Every spirit that speaks isn't the Lord's. His sheep know his voice. Don't be afraid to follow His voice alone. I needed that financial blessing then. If I agreed to wait five years, I would have missed my blessing! Do you know what I do? I see myself as a receptor, sort of having an antenna to the Holy Spirit. I stay in tune with the infinite by peace. If I lose that peace or sense static or a loss of clarity, then I know to be cautious, be aware, use discernment, and stay on track, stay on the channel the Lord has you tuned in to! No one is more grateful than I am to have men or women of God speak into my life, and I've already shown you several times where the word of a prophet or prophetess has freed or blessed me, but I also know if those words are the Lord's words for me, they will be in tune with the infinite within me.

I had a friend on the Cape who was in the Big Brother Big Sister Program. She told me she had met this man who was a "Big Brother" to the brother of the little girl she was a "Big Sister" to!

"I met him at our BBBS picnic. He's such a nice guy. He would be perfect for you!"

"No! No men! I don't want to meet anyone right now. I don't know what it is with me and men, but it never works out."

Others had asked me for dates, and I dated a few I liked, but I just didn't feel led that I should be serious. One persistent man said to me after my telling him no several times and explaining I knew the Lord had someone for me, that I just needed to wait for him.

Being sarcastic, he said, "What do you think, God is just gonna drop someone down from heaven for you?"

I realized right then, "Yes, yes, that's exactly what I believe!"

We both laughed, but somewhere within me, I knew God had my son's father somewhere in the wings for me.

I was renting a big house on Cape Cod with Arika. The house was huge. It was the home of a past surgeon general of the United

States. It was old and beautiful with a staircase that went up the center and then divided into two at the landing on the second floor. It had fireplaces, and hardwood everywhere. It reminded me of a home where you would see the Victorian ladies running around in their long, puffy dresses, while their gentleman friend tied his horse and carriage in the archway outside. It was old but a fun place to live! I could sit in the hallway cove, looking out the window, and see the mill pond in the center of town. On July 4, I had a perfect seat for watching the lighted boat parade on the pond in the little village. I just loved the house and living near the canal. I loved the salt air smell of the ocean and the wind from the sea breeze. No, I wasn't ready to make another mistake in the flesh.

I had made those plenty enough. Though I wanted a man in my life, I would wait. My friend was sure I should meet this "Big Brother" from the program. Several, several times I told her no. We would forget it, and then out of the blue, she would bring him up again. Little did I know, she was working beneath the radar to make certain I met this guy! Because my house was so big, I decided I would rent out rooms and thought this a wise move for me financially. I was a single parent with no support from either one of my ex-husbands. (I know that sounds terrible. One ex is a bad-enough label; two is even more dreadful—especially if you're in the Christian arena—but it is true at that point in my life, I shamefully had two of them. It sure kept pride from my door!) Anyway, renting out rooms sounded like a great idea to help me with my finances. Human service work pays a low wage in the nonprofit field. So my friend who just also happened to be in real estate rentals on the Cape started lining up renters for me! Yes, you guessed it! Months after this BBBS picnic, she sent Jack to my door. The very first encounter with him was God.

I had no idea this man was the man she had been trying to get me to meet for the past six months. I only knew he had an appointment to come and look at my room for rent at 5:00 p.m. that evening. I heard him come up on my porch. This porch is huge, no stoop, as big and spacious as some people's Cape home! So I stood by the over-sized door, looking through the lace that covered the windows alongside of the door, waiting for him to knock. As I looked out, I saw a taller man with Jack, standing behind him, and I thought it odd that he brought someone with him. I slipped away from the window so they wouldn't think I was weird, peeking through the curtain. The doorbell rang. I answered, and there stood Jack, pleasant and Italian as the day is long. I remembered seeing him once at the church I used to attend; he stood out to me. He had gone to a special service the church was having and went forward for prayer for his back. I even remembered what he was wearing the night he went to get prayer. But he was a total stranger to me, and I never saw him again or gave him a second thought. He explained he was there to look at the room that I had for rent, noting that he wasn't quite sure if he wanted to give up his apartment or not; the realtor had sent him.

Formalities were exchanged, and then I asked him, "Where is the man that was with you on the porch?"

He looked bewildered, "What man?"

I said easily, "The tall man who was standing behind you on the porch."

He answered puzzled, "I didn't come here with anybody. I came alone."

Resigning to the reality that he didn't have anyone with him, I breathed, "Oh, okay."

I proceeded to show Jack the house, not just the room for rent. The house was historical and interesting to walk in. It had three levels and a widow's peak where you could see the ocean view. There was a beautiful carriage house in the back and an arched stone canopy attached to the house with the stone steps that were built to allow stepping from a carriage with care. If you walked up those steps, it seemed they walked to nowhere but midair. (You don't see them today; people use cars!) The place was unique but old. It had been vacant for months prior to my renting it. The back stairs led to the servants' quarters that were up on the third floor, which then led up to the widow's peak. The house was filled with history. But it was old. As I gave Jack the tour of the house, we chatted and talked as if we had been friends forever. I told him I remembered seeing him once at a church meeting; he had gone forward for prayer for his back. He remembered that because God touched his back. He wasn't religious, but I knew he knew God.

He jokingly said, "You don't need a renter, you need a maintenance man!" We laughed.

Jack left, and I told him I would be in touch with the realtor. Come to find out, he currently lived within walking distance of my house on the quaint Main Street just down from the library. As soon as he left, I knew there was no way I could rent a room to this man. I knew my flesh, and I was immediately too attracted to him.

I called my friend, the realtor, and told her, "There's no way I can rent to this guy."

When I told her why, she started in, "I told you!"

"You told me what?"

"This is the man from Big Brother Big Sister Program that I've been trying to tell you that you had to meet! I didn't know how else to get you to agree to meet him, so I just arranged for him to come and see the room!"

"Wow, well, you certainly got me on that one! "

We talked for a while, pleasantly laughing and marveling over the whole situation. I even told her about how I had seen someone behind him on my porch!

She said, "This is meant to be, can't you see that?"

I was afraid to see that. So I told her, "Just tell him I'm not renting the room."

I know how weak I am. I know how weak my flesh is. I was lonely, and I preferred to be married, but it seemed that I just always made bad choices, and so I resisted the best I knew how. I would not rent to Jack. I would not see him again, but he had something else in mind. He called me. He didn't care that the room wasn't for rent. He was fine not moving from his apartment. He wanted to know if I would have coffee with him.

At first I said no. I said no several times. He never stopped asking. Then one night, out of the blue, he called and wanted me to go to the movies with him to see *When Harry Met Sally*. I said yes. He was such a gentleman and even stopped on the way to the movie and bought me a rose. I was really very comfortable with him. We talked about everything, hiding nothing from one another: my shame, his shame—no condemnation or judgment—the miracles, the mistakes, the present, the past, the future, all of it. Above all, we talked about wanting a family and not feeling alone. We had coffee dates and walked on the boardwalk and ate at the Marshland Diner, and I met Sammy—Sammy his faithful friend, his yellow Lab.

Sammy even had a part in our getting together. One day, early on in our relationship, Sammy had come to my house with a toy in his mouth, but Jack wasn't with him. I saw him on my porch and let him in my house. He walked over to my dining room table and dropped his toy then made it clear he wanted to go back outside. I let him out, and Sammy left, but he didn't take his toy with him. Of course, I had to call Jack that night and let him know his dog's toy was at my house. When I told Jack the story, he laughed. Sammy wanted Jack to come to my house. It was hard saying no to these two! I'm not sure I could have, even though I tried. Sammy helped me realize that I really loved Jack! Once at Jack's apartment, we were talking about Sam, and Jack told me how Sammy had helped him get sober and help save his life. Jack became very vulnerable to me, exposing that he had done jail time for DUIs—three of them. He fought a hard addiction to alcohol and drugs. He said his dog became his lifeline in some of those times he was using. It was Sam that got him home safely. He knew it was God's way of keeping him alive. His last binge, he ended up in jail, and there someone led him to Christ. When I met him, he was clean and sober for a couple of years.

During this emotional vulnerable conversation, Jack said, "Watch, I'll show you something."

Jack had turned a walk-in closet into Sam's own private room. He had a scripture on Sammy's door, a Proverb that said something about the righteous caring for his animals. He had Sammy go in his room (the walk-in closet), and Jack closed the folding wooden door.

He loudly spoke, "Fire, Sam!"

Sam pushed the door open and ran to the front door! Then Jack explained he had taught Sammy to get out of his room if there was ever a fire so Sam's life would be saved. He actually had fire drills with his dog! How could I not love this man? I did. As much as I tried not to, I did. He was kind and good. He wasn't religious. He was real, and I trusted his heart. Jack fell in love with me too. He introduced me to his parents, and I was invited to Thanksgiving dinner at his parents' home. It would be the first and last Thanksgiving we would have with his mother. She was dying of cancer when I met her.

I became one of her primary caregivers. For the next six months, I would be by her bedside, listening to her life's stories, getting to know her in a very personal way. She shared everything with me. I had no idea I was getting to know my son's grandmother. I only knew I had met this sweet man, Jack, who had a mother dying of cancer, and I was drawn to her, to be there for her. I kept cool cloths on her head. I walked her to the bathroom until she had no strength to walk anymore, then I helped change her and keep her dry and comforted. I spoon-fed her. I sang songs to her, and sometimes during those times when I would just hold her and sing the Word of God and the Psalms over her, she would call me "Momma." I loved her quickly and easily. She had hospice in the end, but up until hospice, she wanted to be in her own home, her own bed, her own way of dying—not a medical way. I was blessed to hear all the stories of her youth and time spent with her sisters, the time she and Mr. Costello met and how they fell in love, how they loved ballroom dancing, and how he knew immediately she was the one for hm. They were married for fifty-plus years when I met them. Once, I remember, when they wanted to start giving her morphine for her pain, she called Mr. Costello upstairs to her bedside. Now this was no easy feat for Mr. Costello. He himself had had a stroke and lost use of his arm and the strength in one of his legs. But his sons helped him up the stairs to their mother's bedside.

I sat by and watched and listened as she said with compromising tone and breath, "What do I do now, John? Should I take it?"

My heart sank. My goodness! My thoughts were, *Here was a couple who knew each other so loving and so well that in her dying breaths, she could trust him with every ounce of her being to help her decide what she should do. I had never seen love like that before.* I thought to myself, *Could you imagine being so loved by someone that they were there faith-*

fully for you until your dying breaths? I had the highest honor and respect for them both.

"Shirl," that's what he called her, "it's okay, take it."

They hugged through tears, and his sons helped him back down the stairs. Her words—"What do I do now, John?"—and what they truly meant to a woman's life have never left my soul. Whatever God meant when He said woman was made for man, this was the closest I had ever come to the purity of it.

Days later, around her bed at the last blessing of their priest, Mrs. Costello spoke to each of her sons. When she spoke to Jack, she took his hand and mine and joined them in spite of her frail state, and she said to her son Jack, "You are one."

We had her blessing, and I knew marriage was ahead for Jack and me. I will never forget the feeling I had as I watched from the upstairs side window and the mortician carried Mrs. Costello's body from her home in the middle of that dark night. I cried like a baby. It was as if I had known her forever, not just six months. I couldn't help but realize this is what the physical life comes to: leaving it all behind—everyone, everything you've ever known—and being carried from your loved ones' lives. At that second, for me, the Holy Spirit hovered, and I knew she lived, though I could no longer see her or hold her. I knew one day I would be reunited in the unseen kingdom with this beautiful lady.

It seemed in my lifetime that I didn't just search for a husband. (I always knew I was "a married wife," even though my lot of it didn't seem the "they lived happily ever after" kind.) It seemed I searched for a family too. I never pretended to be strong in my flesh. I wasn't. Indeed, I was probably one of the weakest women I knew. It seemed important to me to be loved by a man. I know lots of women, my good—even best—friends who don't think that way at all and in fact have never married even once! I have no idea what that feels like. I always knew I was a married woman, and I always knew that I had children and I had my family—my own family, not the kind of family I came from, a family that loved. I believe it's God that made sure I always had both. No matter what the religious people thought, Jack and I married.

Arika was my bridesmaid; Sammy was our ring bearer! Yes, God gave me my son, John. He was finally here! Not without the enemy trying to take him from me, though. What is it that we daily fight the good fight of faith? It's a true saying when someone says, "Keep the faith." We can't live a day without it. Our very breath is the Lord's. Jack and I shared a common bond of wanting a son; that was clear.

It was five o'clock in the morning. Jack and I headed to Falmouth Hospital on Cape Cod with me in labor. Before we left the driveway, though, Jack had to run back in the house to get something. While he was gone and I was sitting in the passenger seat of our jeep, the Lord spoke to me.

He said very clearly, "Whatever you do, don't allow them to induce your labor." That was all He said. I heard it as clearly as if you and I were talking.

When Jack got back out to the jeep, I said to him, "Whatever happens, if I'm unconscious or unable to decide, I want you to know, whatever I do, don't let them induce my labor."

I told him I had heard from God, and I knew I was not to let them induce my labor! He seemed fine with that—at least, up until six hours later, when the doctor said he needed "to induce my labor."

"No! No, I couldn't!"

He did not understand this. The head nurse tried to convince me; the doctor tried to convince me; the RN ahead of my Lamaze class tried to convince me; the RN that changed shifts tried to convince me. They all said that I needed to be induced. They eventually convinced Jack that he needed to convince me to allow this Pitocin. Jack discussed this in private with me. He said the medical team wouldn't accept that I just am saying no for no other apparent reason than I just didn't think God wanted me to take the medicine. He said they thought that was ludicrous and that they wanted him to let me know this was crucial to my health and to the baby's. They convinced him that because my water had broken, time was of the essence. It was crucial for me to take the Pitocin because it would help me deliver quickly, or more quickly.

"No, no, I'm not having my labor induced, no."

"Well, how are you going to explain that you're just saying no?"

"Jack, listen, please, I cannot take this Pitocin. God told me *not* to! I can't fight them and you too. I'm laboring, and I just need you to be on my side. I don't have the strength to keep wrestling over this with them or you. I'm *not* going to have my labor induced, and that is that."

Jack left and went into the privacy of the lavatory. He prayed. He heard God. God told him to do what I wanted and to listen to what I said. He was settled in peace. I would not have my labor induced. The doctors and staff accepted my decision, though they were very upset with me.

At 10:17 p.m. that evening, John Joseph Costello IV weighed in at nine pounds ten ounces by cesarean birth. We have a recording of the delivery. On the tape, you can hear the doctor in awe, speaking to the medical staff with him, grateful—very grateful—that I had *not* allowed my labor to be induced! He clearly states, if I had taken that Pitocin, I could have been lost and our son too, by my uterus erupting with the hard contractions that Pitocin causes. It would have been too much for my uterus! It seemed I had what was called a "window." My uterus was stretched so finely, thinned so much, that the doctor could see right through it and see John's face. The Pitocin would have caused the uterine wall to erupt with the forceful contractions that Pitocin would have brought on. The doctor later spoke with my husband and me, with appreciation that I had heard from God. Again, my God was with me. He is with us all. He just wants us to give back to Him the love He so freely has given to us. That's why we have Jesus. Love.

Arika was happy to get a baby brother; she was sixteen at the time. Her baby brother seemed to slow her down a bit from teenage mischief. She clearly loved the little guy and was proud of him to her friends. Jack and I were in our glory! We both waited so long for this son to come into our lives. Life was good. In time, Arika went on to college in Boston and later met Tim and married. John grew into the blessing the Lord promised he would be. I claimed (and still do) claim every promise the Lord has revealed to me in His Word concerning my children and grandchildren. This promise is to you and to your seed and to your seed's seed. Acts 2:39 says, "For the promise is unto you and to your children, and to all that are afar off, even as many as the Lord our God shall call."

In raising my children, I tried not to expose them to religion. I wanted to expose them to Jesus and His Holy Spirit. I wanted them to know Holy Spirit's presence and be able to discern for themselves what was good and what was not, when He was present and when He was not. This kept my children safe many times. Once, when Arika was with friends and they were drinking at the beach, they all got in the car to go, and Arika heard the Lord say, "Don't get in that car, Arika." She didn't, and it saved her from being in an accident.

Once, when Arika was older, she was driving down the road after leaving church. She saw a group of people around a vehicle on the side of the road and pulled in with concern to see what was happening. As she approached the vehicle, some children ran up to her, yelling, "He's stuck, he's stuck!"

Arika ran over to the crowd and the vehicle, and there in front of her was a child that had been backed over. He was stuck up in the wheel well of the truck. Immediately, Arika called on the Holy Ghost, praying in the Spirit, loudly and audibly! She spoke with other tongues and then gave the interpretation. She declared that this child would live and not die and that the child would not have one broken bone! Immediately, the child was released from the wheel well. He was taken by ambulance to the hospital. A week later, a woman from our church reported that a man had been on that scene where Arika prayed to God and that he saw the miracle of the whole thing. He reported the child was released without one broken bone!

Another time, when a teenage boy threatened Arika and made her afraid, she said she heard me say, "Pray the Lord's prayer out loud, Arika."

I wasn't anywhere near her; I was home! He had taken her to an isolated place and threatened her safety. When she prayed to our Father out loud, the young man plugged his ears and got upset! He couldn't get her home fast enough! These same kind of experiences have happened with John. When he was in places he shouldn't have been, God drew him out of there safely to get him home.

When he was driving his Camaro and hit ice, God protected him when he was driving that same 1985 Camaro from New York to Florida alone. He made it all the way to his sister's driveway in Florida, where the car broke down—not before!—exactly to his destination, where he was safe in his sister's driveway, hundreds and hundreds of miles away.

God leads John, and his relationship is very personal. He has been hurt by religion, and he knows the difference. The Lord is raising him to be a leader. He is a gifted musician, and writer, sensitive to the Spirit. He's radical. Someone once told me, John has been placed at hell's gate to help those who would never enter a church come to know Jesus. I believe that I've seen him do that. He is currently completing his college degree in Entertainment Management, and God is ordering his steps aright!

Arika sadly went through a divorce after twenty years of marriage and a lot of personal opportunities to forgive, until I said no more. I wasn't watching the heartache and brokenness anymore. I moved to Florida for six months. I lived with my son, John, while I helped Arika move into a condo with my grandchildren. The heartache about destroyed her; she was so weakened by it all that she couldn't even get out of bed. God helped carry her through that hard time and allowed me to be there for her and the children (ages ten, eighteen, and twenty).

Eventually, Arika met Brian Edens—Dr. Brian Edens—and God has given her the happiness she deserves. Brian has a son, Chase. Together they all make a beautiful blended family. Tim, my son-in-law, has also grown through this and returned, repentant to the Lord. We talk often and pray for the will of the Lord in his life as well. He is like a son to me. I love him in spite of the reasons for the marriage failing. He will always be like a son to me.

CHAPTER 19

I WOULD LIKE TO TELL you that Jack and I lived happily ever after. I found out there is no such thing. There is the joy of the Lord, and there is the peace that God gives, but the "happy ever after" is for fairy tales, not the tales of one's life journey. It appeared that the stress of taking care of a family and holding a stressful job working as the director of admissions in a drug-and-alcohol rehab eventually buckled Jack.

He fought his own addiction. It returned to haunt him and robbed him of what he had always wanted and lived for. I still had much respect for him, though I was alone again. I know today, years later, he is living a life free from alcohol and street drugs. He loves John more than most fathers I know. He lives alone and is very content with his life. From the time he left, John and I have kept him close to us. Even when I moved from Massachusetts to New York for work, we helped Jack get an apartment near us. He has always been a part of John's life, and I would have it no other way. It proved to be that my move to New York was one of the final transitions in my life but one of the nicest things the Lord could have done for me to show me He understood and knew me. I was never really alone.

I had lost all my ability to even confess that I was a Christian. I mean, come on, really, three breakups and three losses? I happened to be the common factor in that. I felt shame and deep loneliness. Why, why couldn't I just once have a normal relationship? Was I so weak in my flesh that I would get myself into situations that eventually just broke my heart? What was it with me? I was terribly ashamed, and it kept me from opening my mouth about Jesus. I was afraid I'd give Him a bad name—like people would laugh and say, "How could she say she walks with Jesus and go through bad marriages?" I was afraid of giving love a bad name. So I kept quiet. I kept His love to myself and raised my children to know His love, no matter what happens. I didn't share any of the good things the Lord had done in my life. Here I had miracle after miracle, witness of His love and goodness, but I was too ashamed of myself to confess Him to others. I was alone again.

I had to leave human service work; it didn't pay enough to take care of John and me. Jack had gone on disability, so I had to find a better income than human service pay to meet John's and my needs. My brother-in-law got me into a large corporation, and I worked from a temporary employee up to a permanent position—even, in time, becoming a local manager.

The very day that I started my new job during my lunch break, I was on a bridge in Marshfield, Massachusetts, heading back to the store, when my car quit. It just broke down right in traffic on that bridge! The window had a ten-day rejection inspection sticker on it that read clearly, "REJECTION." I sat on that bridge broken down, looking up at that sticker, and the word *rejection* just flooded over me! I felt like I had been rejected my whole life, and this felt like the epitome of it. I started crying. Cars were beeping and moving around me—hurrying, bustling—and instantly, the Lord said to me, "Quit your crying, you have a Volvo!"

Now, here I was broken down in this old Buick, cars honking at me and I was holding up traffic on the bridge, and God told me to quit crying, that I have a Volvo! I was worried that I wouldn't get back on time—my very first day of work on my new job, and what kind of impression that would give my boss. All these things were going through my mind, and the next thing I knew, my car started and I was off the bridge! I was back to work on time, and I was filled with gratitude because I knew the Lord had helped me.

Yes, within weeks, I had a Volvo—a stable, good car that I could get back and forth to work in. I even took more college classes, driving into Quincy, outside of Boston. I kept busy enough for months and years. One day, to my surprise, my mother—my real, biological mother—whom I hadn't seen in I-don't-know-how-long contacted me. She invited me to her home in Pennsylvania. By this time, my stepfather had passed away and Mom lived alone in Starrucca. She told me she wanted me "to come down" and that she wanted me to know that Brent Upright was divorced and why don't I just give him a call and visit him while I'm down there. You remember Brent from the beginning of my story? He was Brian's "little" brother, one of the Upright sons, and we shared a first kiss when we were nine years old! First of all, I was terribly surprised my mother called me.

Secondly, yes, I could come down; I had so much vacation time accrued because I never took time off. I worked all the time to keep my mind and myself busy. Thirdly, yes, that would be nice to see Brent after almost thirty years and just share about life and talk about memories—including our common bond, Brian.

I thought it would be a wonderful break, and yes, I would drive down. I made the arrangements at work and prepared for the weekend with my mother. I thought it would be wise to contact Brent ahead and see if he even remembered me! Then I would let him know I would be coming to Pennsylvania and was there anyway, that I might be able to see him, if he wasn't busy.

Yes, of course, he remembered me!

We talked like old friends do and laughed because I learned he wasn't such a "little" brother after all. He and I were only months apart! I guess, when you're in school, any underclassmen seem so much younger; then you realize, as you age, numbers are a lot closer than you think!

So it was. I would take a "break" and go see my mother and, while there, see Brent. He invited me to dinner Friday evening to meet him at his apartment at 5:30 p.m. He would be out of work by 5:00 p.m.

"Yes, this all sounded just fine, and I will see you then."

I reached my mother's around 2:00 p.m. that following Friday afternoon.

Mom and I had a nice visit. It was good to be back in Starrucca, though it had seriously changed over the past thirty years. It was no longer that quaint little village. The houses were run down. There were no businesses in town now, except for a bed-and-breakfast that functioned on the corner across from the old post office. The stone bridge with its beautiful old arch had been replaced with geometrical straight lines and iron. The farms had closed in the town. The Catholic church where Brian's funeral service was held was empty, shut down by the diocese. Nothing looked the same to me, except the trees and fields.

Mom seemed pleased to see me and was happy that I had made the trip to Pennsylvania. We chatted and talked, getting caught up on the local news and happenings in her life and in Starrucca. She seemed much happier now to me. She actually had a nice male companion that lived in the farm next door, and they went to dinner and to a local coffee house in a nearby town. It was my blessing to see her happy.

When it was time to leave to go meet Brent, Mom was pleasantly pleased that she had made this arrangement possible, and I thanked her for suggesting it.

"It means a lot to me."

"Oh, you just go and have a good time now," she bubbled as I left to find Brent's apartment in the town where we went to school twelve miles away.

I knocked on the door. He answered quickly and with great acceptance in his greeting, smiling, hugging, and I too felt the joy of the moment. How different he looked from when we were kids. I'm sure I did too—though he exclaimed, "You look *fantabulous*!"

I never heard that word. Did he make it up? I found him very interesting, and obviously, he had been working out and had taken care of himself well over the years. His passion was his Harley Davidson! He belonged to a motorcycle club. We left for dinner at a local restaurant and lounge. We got a table in the corner, and we talked and talked and talked! We slow-danced, and something happened. I couldn't tell where I stopped and he started. It was an unreal feeling. I could not distinguish us; we felt like the same person to me. I cried.

After the evening and full conversation, we went back to his apartment. He got out a box of pictures and showed me the past thirty years of his life. We talked about Brian a lot. He said Brian was not the same when he came home on his last leave that he could tell whatever was going on in the war was really getting to him. He was different, not himself; they didn't clown around. He said he had never talked about his brother's death since he was killed. I couldn't believe that! He had kept that in all these years.

He was hurting, and he covered it by drinking, he told me. It's the only way he could handle life and all his feelings. He said his parents never talked about Brian, and it was just understood he was gone. He said he had dreams about him, and once, six years after Brian was gone, he had a dream that Brian was on a school bus, looking out the window at him. It was the first time he had any sense of relief since his death.

I listened intently to all his stories; they came pouring out. He talked as if he hadn't been able to say a word for thirty years! He told me about his failed relationships, and he even told me all the things that made him insecure and personal things that he judged himself for and the things that made him feel ashamed and guilty. He didn't have to do that; he owed me nothing. But it was like a catharsis for him. He kept talking.

By 4:00 a.m., I had to get back to my mother's. When we were saying good-bye, Brent asked if I could stay a day longer and attend a party with him Saturday night at a friend's home. I said okay, yes, I could stay. There wasn't any urgency for me to be back home Saturday night. So we parted ways with plans to meet that evening. Mom was good about letting me sleep in the next morning. She was even happier that I was going to stay another night. She made me feel welcomed in her home. I did meet Brent the next evening, though this time, he picked me up at Mom's. She was happy to see him too. It had been a lot of years! Brent and I left for the party. I met all his biker friends.

His lifestyle was quite different from mine. But they were all nice people, just different from what I was used to being around! I realized it was a good thing he asked me to stay. His friend's girlfriend had invited a girl from Buffalo to come down to the party with the intention of meeting Brent!

It was a disappointment to her that he had brought a date! I was wondering what all this was going to lead to? I would be leaving to go back to Massachusetts the next day, and he would carry on in his biker lifestyle in Pennsylvania. We had another precious evening talking, dancing, reminiscing our youth and our lives. I felt fully human, fully alive. I enjoyed every minute with him.

On Sunday before I headed back to the Cape, he met my mother and me at the fire hall in Thompson. They were having a chicken biscuit dinner. Everybody I knew from Starrucca was there! It was like old home day. I enjoyed the atmosphere and the gathering so much. When we finished our dinner and went back to Mom's, I was packing my car, getting ready to head back to the Cape. I started crying, realizing how precious all the time shared had been. Brent had a going-away present for me. He bought a large blue ocean breeze candle for me; that made me cry more. He just held me in my mother's front lawn as I cried against his chest.

He said, "What's wrong? It wasn't that bad, was it?"

He made me laugh. I told him he made me feel like I had found something I had lost long ago—like I spent a lifetime looking for a needle in a haystack and I found it but had to leave it all behind. We parted ways, both saying we would stay in touch. I returned to my work and to my busy life, but nothing felt the same. My birthday was near, and I received a dozen red roses that came to my place of work for me. The card said, "Love Always, Brent."

When communicating, he had invited me down to share Thanksgiving at his sister's with his parents and family. He also asked if I would escort him to his company's Christmas party in December. He obviously was thinking ahead. Of course, I said yes to both. What was happening? Did I dare have feelings about this? After seeing Brent the first time, I had a dream—the last dream I have ever had about his brother Brian.

In the dream, Brian had walked through a door and up to the table I was sitting at. In the background, there was hammering and pounding, as if someone was building something. It seemed they were getting ready for a wedding! Brian walked by my table, and I looked at him and said, "I can't marry you, Brian. I'm in love with your brother Brent." Brian gently smiled and nodded yes, and then as gently as he entered through the door, he was gone. I couldn't admit to myself I loved Brent, but in my dream, I knew I did. It was only weeks, and I wondered how could we ever be together; our lifestyles weren't even similar. When I spoke of spiritual things to Brent, he didn't reject what I shared, but he didn't really understand it either. He had a seat at the local bar frequented so often they labeled it Brent's chair and would move to let him have it! The motorcycle rides ended up hopping from bar to bar. All this did not settle for a lasting relationship. I certainly had been through enough to know that. What would God say? He did speak to me about Brent. He told me to see him as innocent, not to hold anything against him. I was to look at him as pure as a child, the way the Lord sees us! What? Okay, God! That alone kept me believing for Brent's salvation, regardless of any behaviors. I wrote a letter to Brent, admitting that I loved him, and I said, "If you don't love me, let me go right now, because I realize you have power to hurt me. I don't want to be invested and find out down the road it was all a mistake."

Brent did love me. He and I stayed in touch, having a long-distance relationship. In time, Brent too accepted Jesus as his Lord. When he was baptized, he told the Lord that he would only drink socially and that he would never ever be drunk again. God did one up on him, though. He took away every desire of Brent's to drink. He didn't want to drink at all, and he hasn't. He quit smoking cigars. He stopped hanging out in places that were not healthy for him. He was serious about accepting Jesus as his Lord and his savior. The Lord healed his body from eczema; the Lord healed his knee. The Lord has spoken to him, telling Brent "to seek His face." Brent has; he has a hunger for God that runs deep. Brent and I married. He is the most stable, consistent, dependable man a woman could ever know. We've been together going on twenty years, and he's as loving now to me as he was that first dinner we shared. The Lord has given us a beautiful home and a steadfast love for one another. I saw Brian smile on us in my dream. I know God smiles on us. Brent has two adult girls and three grandchildren. He is kind and generous to them and prays regularly for their lives. Together, Brent and I have labored for the kingdom. We served as pastor to two churches for several years. We held weekly Bible studies in our home. Currently, I hold a women's Bible group once a month in our home. I'm on the ministry team of the Remnant Sons of God and the Remnant Sons Motorcycle Club, serving as a spiritual mentor to them. I am happy. I am a married woman. I am blessed with the family the Lord has given me—my daughter, my son, and my grandchildren.

I am blessed that only a loving Father would see the child within me and lead me all the way home.

I am blessed that the Lord would send a man like Brent—of course, yes, Brian's brother—to be my husband. I am blessed that God would not allow shame to bind me. I am blessed. I AM an EAGLE in the kingdom!

CHAPTER 20

I WAS A YOUNG WOMAN when Kathryn Kuhlman left the earth and went to be with the Lord in the '70s. I remember it as if it were yesterday. I was working the midnight shift at the factory down in what they called the catacombs. It was an isolated dark spot in the glassworks. This night I didn't mind being down there and alone because I was sincerely grieving Ms. Kuhlman's death. I cried. I cried out to God from that isolated place.

"Lord, to whom will they go now? Who will be there for them? Who will stand in her place for you? Who will show them Jesus?"

My heart ached for the people who needed her still, people who needed a touch of the Holy Ghost's presence. I knew her holy fire. I had drawn from her early in my salvation. I made a declaration before God and said, "Lord, if you can ever use me for your glory as you used Ms. Kuhlman, I offer myself to you."

That was it. I missed her like you would miss a friend or a sister. I loved her because I knew how much she loved God, and I knew the price she paid to serve Him. She had my utmost respect in Christ. I saw Jesus in her. I could identify with her holy fire.

In 2008, I attended the revival in Florida. I took three other women from our church, and we drove from New York to the revival. I personally went to seek the Lord and to separate myself unto Him, with others calling out to Him at that time. I was ready for the refreshing of the Lord; I was ministering in two churches at the time. The break was a welcomed one. We stayed in the hotel that was at the same airport as the revival, which was really nice because the meetings were easily accessible to us. I had many personal encounters with God during that time there, but the one that has changed my destiny was this one. If you have ever been under my ministry, this encounter has changed your life too.

There were a recorded ten thousand people in this huge airport terminal. Worship would go on for hours there. This one night after worship at the altar and just prior to the message being given, I was standing at my seat in the Lord's presence. I looked up at the throng of people going to their seats from the altar after worship. My eyes saw this one man, and it was as if the Lord had placed a tag on him or something.

I could relate to Samuel choosing David. Something had related in my soul to this man as soon as I saw him; it was as if I knew him already. I wondered to myself, Was he somehow my brother? Was he somehow related to Brent and Brian? What was this? What connection did we have? He passed my seat, and we only exchanged a glance—like the hundreds of others returning to their seats after worship—but there was more to it, and I knew it in my spirit. The following day, I was sitting by the outdoor pool at the airport hotel, talking with a crowd of people. The Spirit of the Lord was present as I shared the testimony of Jesus healing my child. Several souls were touched: a pastor and his wife from England, a group of women from Texas who were there for the revival also staying at the hotel, a minister who took me aside to tell me the Lord was going to use His anointing in me. As I looked up across the pool on the other side, there was the man from the tent. I could not believe it. Was he in the same hotel as we were?

Obviously, he was, so I decided to approach him. I told him I had seen him the evening before in the tent. He recalled also seeing me in spite of the hundreds of people. We briefly exchanged greetings and talked about how amazing the Lord's presence has been during the week of prayer and revival. He shared that he was in a motorcycle ministry and was seeking the Lord for clarity about it. It seemed he felt the compromise of the club shifting from Jesus being the focus, and it burdened him. He wanted a motorcycle ministry where Jesus was first then the club. He knew he was an end-time warrior. That was it! That is what I totally related to in him! I knew the warrior in him; one warrior for the kingdom knows another! You would find us radical for the spirit of truth—not typical, not a religious expression, but a war cry of truth. He shared how he felt, as if he knew me somehow too. I knew it was the warrior in us! He told how he had become saved and how the ministry of Nicki Cruz affected his life for Christ—something he could relate to *The Sword and the Switchblade*. He had been in gangs as a teen on the streets in the city of Pittsburgh. He had learned early to defend himself and had to be tough to make it on the streets. He now carried that as a warrior for Christ. I could relate. He told me about his wife, Deb, how they have been together since they were kids and she too was serving the Lord, helping people and giving to the poor and supporting ministries for the kingdom's sake. We parted ways at the poolside, knowing Christ in one another. We thought that was it, a visit for two warriors by the pool. God had something else in mind.

A few days passed. On the final Sunday of my visit to the revival, I decided to stay and attend the church service they were offering in the hotel. The ladies with me also joined me in the service. There was a couple, a husband and wife, that held the meeting. However, they had a guest from Australia sharing the Word at the beginning of the service. He spoke briefly, approximately ten minutes, and the Holy Spirit was so strong upon him and so powerfully moving through him that I could not believe they had him sit down and did not let him hold the entire service! To me, he was like a fresh, living well gushing clear holy water, and then they just capped it! They took over the service, and it was not the same. My thought was that I did not drive the whole east coast hundreds of miles to attend a dry service. So I left and returned to my hotel room with the other women who were with me.

When I returned to my room, the Lord spoke clearly to me and said, "There is a prophet in the house. He who honors a prophet receives a prophet's reward."

I told the ladies what I heard; together we went to find the man who had originally spoken at the service. I knew he was the prophet the Lord was speaking to me about. I waited in the hallway of this huge hotel and was going to address the man of God when he came out of the service. Interestingly enough and to my surprise, there was the "warrior" also waiting in the hallway for this man of God. I didn't know it at the time because I had left the service early, but this prophet spoke to this warrior and told him to wait for him in the hallway as the Lord had something for him! So here we were, that warrior brother and myself, waiting in this huge hallway, hundreds of miles from our homes by order of the Lord! When he came out of the service, I told him what the Lord had said to me!

He introduced himself and said he was a prophet from Australia! He held a prayer service right there in that hallway for this little group that was sent to him! He prayed for the women first, and when he prayed for us, he placed the "warrior" behind me with instructions for him to place his hand on my head. When this warrior brother, Les, prayed over me, I immediately felt the fire I knew from the Kathryn Kulhman Ministry! What? How could this be? It circled my head like a ring of fire. We all received prayer, and that man of God prayed over Les and declared him as a leader in a ministry, calling him a "screaming eagle!"

Little did this man know that Les's motorcycle was a screaming eagle and that Les was seeking clarity about the motorcycle ministry! He connected Les and me at that time and declared to us we were warriors for the kingdom's sake—a total confirmation of what God had placed in my heart, coming from a man from Australia who did not know Les nor me from Adam! Later, I learned that Les had been brought up in Pittsburgh under the Kathryn Kuhlman Ministry and that his son, Larry, had been baptized by Ms. Kuhlman. This was nothing Les and I could have put together. It was God. We have been in ministry since Les in Pittsburgh, I in New York.

Then in 2010, The Remnant Sons of God Motorcycle Club formed, having chapters in different states all over the United States. I became a spiritual mentor and intercessor for the ministry; my husband became a chapter president at that time. The ministry continues to grow and expand to this day—changing "mere men" into "men of God"; warriors for the kingdom, ready "to fight a good fight of faith"; preparing for and looking for, uncompromisingly, the return of Jesus in an end-time move of God! These men are transformed by the renewing of their mind, taken from the depths of self and conformed into the image of Christ. With the Remnant Daughters, they serve the poor, the homeless, the broken and bruised, the addicted, the lost, the cheated, the despised, and the imprisoned. They love the sinner and lead them back to Jesus—not through religion, but through a heart that loves as Jesus would love. They serve at the Easy Rider Rodeos, giving tirelessly of themselves and selflessly are lights in a dark world. Many miracles and transformed lives have come out of this group. Other ministries have joined the mission under The Remnant Sons of God, and together stand for Jesus, like the remnant warriors we are for such a time as this! The beauty of it is that there is no way man did this. God took a man from Pennsylvania and a woman from New York who never would have met, led them to Florida, and had a prophet from Australia speak into their lives for the kingdom.

He confirmed that meeting by a holy fire that consumes me and has been my heart's cry here on earth! I am where I belong. I am fulfilling my reason to live, joined by the wailing women who pray with me.

I have taken you through my life, exposing my sin and my redemption. There are many miracles Jesus has done in my life, and through my ministry, I could not number all that He has done for me. But I started this book with a scripture from the Psalms that says, "Teach us to number our days and incline our hearts to wisdom." My heart's desire is that you will hear the voice of the Lord in the pages of this book and realize we are not just a ball of earth floating around a huge star in a cosmic arena.

We have been created by love. God is love and is there for you. Understand, the devil is here and real, not a joke. Know that he walks about spiritually, like a roaring lion seeking whom he may devour. Know that you have been given power through the blood of Jesus to overcome him who is the prince of the power of the air here on earth. Know that the preaching of the cross is foolishness to those who do not believe, but it is the power of God to those who do believe and called to be sons of God! Above all, I hope that you will realize you are a spirit being, not a physical being only—made in the image of God, Who created you. I pray you will come to know yourself by knowing Jesus and that you will use the gift within you for His sake. I pray that at His return (because He is returning), He will find faith in your heart for Him at His appearing. I encourage you to seek. Leave the world behind, and follow Jesus.

I'm leaving you with the words Jesus said to Arika when He healed her and sent her back to me. They are His words: "All I want you to do is love me."

I write this book; I say the words. I tell you for Him because I have learned, there is nothing that compares to loving Jesus and being loved by Him—nothing.

I also leave you with the words the messenger gave me when Brian was killed: "Jesus has a reason for you."

Find your reason for being alive. I bless you in the name of the Father and the Son and the Holy Ghost. I will see you in the kingdom!

Update—today Mr. and Mrs. Upright still live in the little village of Starrucca. The bears visit their backyard, and they get great enjoyment from the birds they feed and the garden they tend.

Brenda Upright Reddon is married to Bob Reddon. They have a son, Bill. They have blessed Brent and me in many ways. We favor them; their hearts are open books. I love you Brenda and Bob; your love towards me has made a difference in my life.

Brett Upright is a miracle. He was hit by a bus at an intersection and was a victim of a TBI (traumatic brain injury). He had to learn all over again how to walk, talk, and think logically. He is precious and very sincere, a lot of fun, and a pleasure to share life with. We have deep love for him.

Brad and Jeanne Upright live in Pennsylvania with their two daughters and sons-in-law, Chandra and Bill, Erika and Mark. They have been blessed with a beautiful family and gifted amazing grandchildren.

Brent's daughters, Michele and Daniele, live in Pennsylvania and are happily raising their families.

They have blessed Brent with three adorable grandchildren, Paeton, Malaki, and Izaiah and have made him a proud grandpa! Michele has a companion, Jason, who also is a part of our life.

Dyke and Zilla Cook live in a beautiful home in the New York Mountains. They have two adult children, Renaye and Greg—both of whom have married good life partners, adding blessed grandchildren to their family. I had the privilege of officiating Renaye's daughter's wedding. They all remain in my heart.

John, my son, graduated from State College of Florida and is currently attending the University of Central Florida, majoring in Entertainment Management. He is personal, unique, a great communicator, cool, and loves the Lord. He is a gifted songwriter, composer, and musician. He lives life with purpose. He played his music in church for months and realized that isn't his calling; now he plays in coffeehouses, pubs, or where he is invited. Jack, his father, lives nearby and is an important part of our lives and always will be. John's grandfather, Mr. Costello, has passed away, but his sons and their beautiful families thrive and are a goodly heritage to his name.

Arika, my daughter, is living in Florida and is a realtor. She also works at the Waterlefe Golf and River Club in Bradenton, Florida. She has started a college path toward law.

She has met the most sincere man, Dr. Brian Edens. He clearly honors and adores her, and that blesses a mother's heart! They have a blended family—Chase, Nick, Luke, and Ava. My granddaughter, Ava, is an avid softball player. She has played for years, traveling all over Florida for competition. Her dream is to attend college on a softball scholarship. Arika has remained cancer free because Jesus *is* Lord!

Gene, Arika's father, lives in the little town we graduated in. He has two sons, Chris and Tyler—which means Arika has three brothers (of course!), and Gene and I remain friends to this day.

Les and Debbie Schnepp continue to work for the Lord in the ministry of the Remnant Sons. They have two adult children (Micki and Larry) and a daughter-in-law, Jennifer—one of the kindest, sweetest families I know, blessed with Jack, a grandson. He lights up their lives with love!

In spite of the abuse we all lived in, my oldest brother Benn led a productive life in the Air Force for many years, retiring and then working for the government, on the Island of Diego Garcia in the Indian Ocean. He has passed away since this writing. His wife remains and his sons and daughters, also giving him many grandchildren and great-grandchildren.

Benn has left me with many good memories of how a big brother loves his little sister.

My oldest sister, Becca, is a rag-to-riches story. She became one of the top realtors in her state, and in her lifetime, she and my brother-in-law designed and had their dream home built. They are blessed with two adult children and several adorable grandchildren—one of which has recently made my sister a great-grandmother! They are good Christians and love the Lord.

My sister Sarra is retired with her faithful husband, who is a gifted artist. He too designed and built their home—a beautiful three-story log house in the mountains. They are blessed with three adult children and wonderful grandchildren and great-grandchildren. They clearly add love and peace to my sister.

My brother Gandy, the "Gandy Dancer," has my heart. The memories of our childhood together are etched in my soul. He will always be special to me; we have a close relationship. He and his wife are retired and have the luxury of six months North and then six months South, escaping the cold! I have two nieces and a nephew and several greats through him. I also have an ex-sister-in-law, who is precious to me as the mother of my nieces and nephew. I am sorry to say, due to my mother's dysfunction, she caused a great divide in our family among my siblings in later years. Mother, by her insensitivity to ever acknowledge the hurt she contributed to her daughters, added salt to their wounds by overlooking all her girls in her will—singling out one child—and this too added a serious fracture to our family. It's all ashes to me. The pain that bound us as siblings growing up is a tie that binds me to them all. They are special people, who excelled in life in spite of horrendous abuse. We all could have ended up dysfunctional to ourselves and to society, but God's grace is greater!

My mother, Dorothy, passed away in a nursing home. I was with her weeks at a time at the facility, staying by her side. I took a family leave of absence and vacation time and traveled the few hours from our home to her. I gave her communion two weeks before she passed in order for her to search her heart and mind. She had me call my sisters and speak to them for her, though the bridge was never really mended. She preferred a stranger do her eulogy, a pastor she didn't even know, rather than have me do it. She really never knew me. I would have been merciful toward her and spoke with compassion and the good in spite of the abuse we all knew. I saw her as a victim of domestic violence and a life that was filled with one tragedy after another, rather than as a mother who couldn't nurture. I honor her simply because she is my mother, and I miss her. I miss what we never had. I did have the honor of being with her right up to the end. I had gotten to the nursing facility after celebrating John's sixteenth birthday. Then making the two-hour trip to her, I went to her bedside. When I got there that evening, the nursing staff told me that she had been unresponsive all day and was growing weaker. However, it seemed she knew when I arrived and kissed her.

She woke and with compromised breath said, "Tell them to give me my medicine, you adjust my fan, and sing to me, Mary Pat."

I sang for four hours well into the late night until I knew the restlessness was gone and she seemed peaceful. She died that day—only in body, though—but to this day remains in my heart and always will.

My father, Francis, died young due to repercussions of alcoholism. I did do his eulogy, and I honored him for being my father in spite of his addiction. I knew he was pleased with the honor I gave him. He had a daughter present at his funeral that was a sister my brother Gandy and I never met until three years before Dad's death. She affected his life in a good way, and because of her, he stopped drinking, living the last three years of his life sober. I was grateful to get to know him in a sober state because of her.

After Dad's funeral, a man walked up to me—who also battled alcoholism—and said to me, "I hope when I die, someone will pay the honor to me and say the things about me that you said about your father." He was crying.

After Dad's eulogy, my Aunt Trese told me she could see me "as an author, a New York best seller." It made me feel guilty that I ever doubted her love for me. After all, it was her good life that showed me how people who weren't poor lived. I wanted mine to be orderly like hers; it was the conflict of loyalty within a child's heart that made me unsure of it all. I realize I was blessed to have Aunt Trese.

Finally, last but not least, Brian Upright is buried in the Pleasant Mount Cemetery in the mountains of Pennsylvania, in his family's plot. His body has been there since he was nineteen; his spirit has not. I never went to the grave site after Brian's funeral. I couldn't stand the thought of his name engraved in a stone in a cold cemetery. But one sunny spring day thirty-plus years later, his brother Brent—my husband—took me on a motorcycle ride, and together we went to Brian's grave site and thanked him for giving us "love."

I close with a dream God gave me last night. Here it is.

A little boy had done something that his father had to correct him for. The father sat the child next to him after scolding him.

The little boy looked up at his father and said, "Daddy, I'm mad at you, but hold me like I'm *not* mad at you."

So it is with our heavenly Father and us. He will never stop holding us. With this thought, forgiveness in this life—whether you yourself have been abused, cheated on, lied to, humiliated, denied love from, treated unjustly, rejected, lived through tragedy or addiction, whatever the case—forgiveness is a gift of God: the Lord's forgiveness to us and then our ability to forgive ourselves and others. Love covers sin, and love never stops calling. Until you see Him face-to-face, stay "wise as a serpent, harmless as a dove" (Matthew 10:16, KJV). Don't be afraid to be you; take off the masks and all pretenses, and be free in Jesus. Know Him, and be known by Him. I'm telling you all this for Him and you. I pray you see Jesus.

I leave you with the blessing of my Lord Jesus Christ, author and finisher of my faith.

I cried as I wrote the end of my book because all my life, this story has been within me. To see it on paper, tangible, the unseen to the seen, stirs the Ghost of God within me because I know the testimony of my daughter being healed of cancer will still be told in years to come through these pages.

I know that whoever Brian Upright is, he has been a gold thread throughout my lifetime on earth. I am honored to be the wife of Brent Upright, who loves me the way Brian Upright would have wanted the abused child he knew and protected, loved. I'll retire knowing true love and loyalty from a husband, by God's grace that worked in my life.

That's who we are.

I hope *you* are the one that has had your faith kindled and your love for Jesus stirred by my story.

Thank you ... I'll see you in the His kingdom!

"Come quickly Lord Jesus."

You may contact me for ministry at *Kellyangel53@aol.com*

ABOUT THE AUTHOR

Mary Patricia Kelly Upright has always been intrigued by words, *Night Blooming (Serious) Cereus Cactus* and *Flatbottom Clouds* are among her favorite! Born at home in the 1950s, she could always appreciate the simple beauties of life and found serene pleasure in the woods, fields, and creeks of the Pennsylvania mountains. Her peace in life has come from her faith, and it is her desire that if anyone remembers anything about her after her death, it's that they are able to say of her, "She was a woman of faith." She currently lives in upstate New York with her husband, Brent. The gifts of her life are her daughter, Arika, and her son, John, and her three grandchildren—Nick, Luke, and Ava. All of whom have given her life deeper meaning and great satisfaction as a mother and grandmother. Some of her most cherished moments are the times shared with her family—whether it's listening to her son's creativity of word and music, rafting down the Delaware River, touring Ringling Brothers Museum, attending plays at the theater, always the holidays at home, or her granddaughter as a toddler sitting on her lap at story time to read—"Not out of the books, Gramma, tell me your stories, tell me about Madeline" (Madeline, Gramma's made-up story). Graduating from Cape Cod College in Barnstable, Massachusetts, receiving an associate's degree, and graduating magna cum laude from Binghamton University in Vestal, New York—Mary Pat received her bachelor's degree in Human Development. Her passion is the Remnant Sons of God Ministry and the adventures of living life in the spirit!

CPSIA information can be obtained
at www.ICGtesting.com
Printed in the USA
LVHW041130250219
608657LV00001B/152